Fresh Grass

32 Independent Poets

Edited by Roseanne Ritzema

D1522686

PRESA 9/10
SPRING/FALL, 2009

ACKNOWLEDGMENTS

First Edition

Printed in the United States of America

ISBN: 978-0-9800081-6-6

PRESA :S: PRESS
PO Box 792   Rockford, Michigan 49341
presapress@aol.com   www.presapress.com

Editorial Comments

This anthology presents generous selections from the works of the most frequently published contributors to issues 1-8 of *Presa*. During the first 4 years of *Presa*, a canon of poets emerged. They rose like cream to the top of our cups, not only through their contributions to *Presa*, but in their participation in the independent literary scene as a whole. These are poets with established reputations whose work has been published primarily in the best indie literary journals such as *Bogg, Chiron Review, Gargoyle, HazMat Review, Home Planet News, Iconoclast, The New York Quarterly, Poesy & Rattle*, as well as in numerous smaller magazines of equal quality such as *Barbaric Yawp, Big Scream, Free Verse* & *Ibbetson Street*. Webzines such as *Napalm Health Spa, The Pedestal* & *Wilderness House Literary Review* spread their seeds to fertilize fields around the globe.

These poets hail from every region of America. Their day-jobs range from bartender to farmer, from college professor to social worker, from printer to technological advisor. Their literary work is nurtured by real life experience that cannot be had in a school at whatever level. These poets come from a vantage point outside the academy. They are each others editors & contributors. Every poet has also been or is currently an editor, proactive in the small press movement.

Although divergent in style, these poets share a mutual respect & community values. Putting style aside, one might say that these poets are in the Whitmanic tradition. They write in the colloquial vernacular. Each expresses an internally original music, personal yet universal. For these poets, form arises naturally from content, & imagery is evocative. Each poet opens a different door of perception to the reader, using many keys, involving the reader in the experience of the poem. They bridge the communication gap at a primary level. Too creative for schools, they are united in their independence, the true successors to the Beats, but more creative in range. In the words of the immortal bard:

> *"This is the grass that grows wherever the land is and the water is. This is the common air that bathes the globe."*

> from *Song Of Myself*
> - Walt Whitman

In memory of
Dave Church.
His contribution mattered.

Contents

6

JOHN AMEN

History

i.

The detective whispers to the nun,
seven girl scouts held hostage in a library.

Poodles are snarling in the boxwood maze.

I spent the morning sharpening knives, filing
family photographs, tried on my grandfather's wingtips.

I am still channeling, sweetheart.

ii.

This is the second time I have
swallowed my tongue during a meditation.

If you were here, I would show you my teeth.

Yellow stain on the confession gown.
An owl beating its wings in the belfry.

The composer shreds his tablature.
Fire in the wheat. The farmer signs the contract.

iii.

A faint ticking sound in the tunnel;
again my guts on the rotisserie of blame.

Our ambition
is what the minotaur really wants.

My love, somehow you are always
two or three steps ahead of me, so well
you wield the plane, hammer, balance.

iv.

The jester is squatting by the hydrant.
He brings old news to the gateway of awe.

There is a crack in the chandelier.

I'm made of fairy tales, thorns, grapes as ripe as justice.

Must there always be an interpreter?

I hereby attest to
the malevolence of the atom.

v.

Ironweed spreads
Azalea, crimson dragon, snorting in its trench

I forget, are the clocks racing or lagging?
What story unfolds behind the opaque window?
Who is inside, patching meaning
onto the holey rags of illusion?

Performing communion in the television glow?

Gorging to keep cruel hours at bay?

vi.

After the pulping of sky, mud.
I denied my roots a dozen times. A pro
gave me a valentine and wished me well.

The renderer stepped away from his churn.
A process of elimination began.

Surgeons. Stickmaen whistling in the rain.
Your children turning over our birdbaths.
So many hawks frozen in the pines.

In the end, everything seems like theater.

the women at the breakfast table
for my sisters

the women at the breakfast table alternate roles—each morning one is the harlot, one the histrionic, and one the sage, they learn to play the parts impeccably, working with proven scripts, improvising when it seems appropriate, the harlot speaks of her desire, fellatio and cunnilingus, the men she has met in stores and restaurants and movie theaters, the histrionic wails about her misfortunes, injustices she must contend with, she pulls her hair out, scratches her face, weeps until her eyes are swollen and red. the sage cultivates equanimity, volunteering aphorisms, refusing to get ruffled, she meditates at an altar, takes long walks on the beach, the women age and eventually retire, they pass on the practice to their daughters, who pass it on to their daughters, who have now passed it on to you.

in the course of things

i convert my family home into a rehab and begin taking in addicts. i blackmail my mother into doing the cleaning, threatening to tell the town about her dabblings in palmistry. she dusts and polishes with a frown. i recruit my ingénue, who comes by daily, offering lectures on body awareness and salvation. she puts on a good face, but i know she would rather be back at the ranch, riding her favorite horse at dawn, tending the vegetables. she and my mother begin to commiserate, complaining of my negligence, my mother soon speaks exclusively in the old tongue, which i never learned. she teaches it to my ingénue, teaches her the black gestures, the ancient spells. i throw myself deeper into my work. then: i'm counseling this kid from California, a real cutter. all the while my ngénue and mother are pacing the balcony, mumbling imprecations, hissing like a couple of incorrigible vipers. i rise and with one motion blind my mother, turn my ingénue into a ceramic swan. now my mother prays as she cleans. a month ago, one of the addicts knocked over the swan statue, shattering it on the floor, i'm using the fragments in the bottoms of flowerpots, to help with drainage.

passage

i drove to the station at the end of my mind and stopped to get gas. a blind man with a stick kept banging around, trying to find his way to the sidewalk. i swiped my credit card, and the pump began beeping, plumes of

13

smoke spewing from the nozzle. cops appeared and put a boot on my car. i ran inside to find the cashier, who was playing scrabble with a rabbi. "what should i do about my car?" i yelled. "help me spell a six-letter word using the letters x, u, and f," the rabbi said. the cashier swatted a fly and downed a can of ginger ale. i stormed out and walked to the road. with each step, darkness grew thicker. a limo finally came by, stopped, and i climbed in. "you're right on time," the driver said. "yeah, i'm good that way," i replied. the driver stomped the accelerator, and we soared into the night. i stripped my clothes off, hurled them out the window into the void. the driver started to hum, some ancient melody that sounded vaguely familiar. we didn't say anything for hours, but i could have sworn, somehow, that i'd known her all my life.

Missive #2

My marathon days are now a matter of record
with the proper Goliaths. I agree, red is ecumenical.
God hath blessed our hunches. I promise to adore
this saccharine pill. Oh, you and your rectitude.
I remain unimpressed with the snake-handling constituency,
though I do, Ms. Clean, pity your concupiscent daughter.
Safety in numbers, after all. Announcements, alas,
are not my area of expertise. Please, tenure someone
who puts water before theory. In that sense, our tongues
are forever minor. Find respite in parabolas and mauve.
I swell and blister in morning light. Keep your bones strong.
Don't lie with eavesdroppers. Check equipment for lice.
If questioned, you're advised to swallow my name.

Missive #8

Sickness is a bad boat gone belly-up. I can,
however, contribute jasmine. Ancillary note:
I worship only the clown within. Nothing
certainly warrants repeating. You'll find
my pipes in the daffodil bed. I think all paths
lead to rape. No need for remonstrance, we'll
reissue the hyacinths, dedicate three Fridays
to your vision of hemlock and vanilla beans.
I'm giving notice regarding lyrics, conversion,
and peanut butter. I'm dead until you tender

the word. Background usually becomes foreground.
Weeds remind me of sad maestros. What burns
burns as fake as Christmas. Veiled, like you.

ANTLER

The Size Of Milwaukee

If the Sun takes up 99.9% of the matter
       of the Solar System,
And if all the planets, moons, asteroids and comets
       take up 1/10th of 1%,
The Earth, after the total of all the matter
       of the Sun
And all the matter of the comets, asteroids, moons and planets
       is taken into account,
Represents only one millionth of 1%
       of the matter of the Solar System,
And if you take away all the space between
       the electrons and the nucleus
Of all the atoms that comprise
       the matter of the Earth
It turns out 99% of the Earth is actually
       empty space,
It turns out the Earth is actually
       the size of Wisconsin,
Wisconsin is actually
       the size of Milwaukee,
And Milwaukee is actually
       the size of a poppyseed!

Doesn't Have to Believe to Be Born

A baby in the womb
    doesn't have to believe
        its Mother exists
    to be born.
A baby inside its Mother
    doesn't have to believe
        it's inside its Mother

to be born.
A baby in utero
    doesn't have to believe
        it will be born
    to be born.
An unborn baby
    doesn't have to believe in
        life after birth
    to be born
        grow up
    live long
        life before death.
A baby in the womb
    doesn't have to believe
        in God to be born
    in a savior to be born
        in a soul to be born
    in immortality to be born
        in heaven to be born.
Baby in the womb
    one night,
Next night
    baby nursing
        in its Mother's arms.

The Twinkle

If there can be a twinkle in the eye
    why not a twinkle in the nose
        or a twinkle in the anus?
Why not a twinkle in the orgasm?
If a mother says to her young son
    once he was the twinkle
        in his father's eyes,
If a father says to his young son
    once he was the twinkle
        in his mother's eyes
And if the spark of their eyes
    and fused thighs
        kindled his life,
Was there not a twinkle
    in their balls and ovaries?

Was there no twinkle
        in their cock and pussy?
Was there no twinkle
        in their orgasm?
No twinkle
        in their toddler's tinkler
                as it tinkles?
No twinkle
        in tow-headed son's
                boyish wetdream?
If Rip van Winkle laughs
        he's got so many wrinkles
                his wrinkles have wrinkles,
Can't a poet have so many twinkles
        his twinkles have twinkles?
Can't there be a twinkle
        in a girl's budding breasts?
Can't there be a twinkle
        in the lubricant drop at the tip
                of a boy's erect dick?
So you don't believe in God,
So you don't believe in Christ,
So you don't believe in the Soul.
Well, what do you believe in?
        The twinkle.

Meant Something 300 Years Ago

When a bomb the size of a poppy seed can blow up a plane,
When a bomb the size of a pumpkin seed can blow up a train,
When a bomb the size of a peanut can blow up a skyscraper,
When a bomb the size of a football can blow up a city,
When a bomb the size of a police car can blow up a State,
When a bomb the size of a skyscraper can blow up the Earth,
Then, when tsunamis of terrorists flood America
        coast to coast,
When no second passes without a girl or boy
        blowing themselves up
                to kill innocent bystanders,
What future for ever-increasing profit margin then
        when the very existence of money
                is in contempt of court,
When a man can by blowing his brains out
        kill not only himself
                but everyone on Earth

the entire Earth and
                    the endless Universes
          pastpresentfuture
                    in a nanosecond?
You're telling me a child sticking out his tongue
          to catch a snowflake makes a difference?
You're telling me a girl turned on by her girlfriend's
          breasts makes a difference?
You're telling me an eagle feather on a mountaintop
          meant something 300 years ago?
You're telling me God wants everyone
          to grow old and die
Because Eve ate the apple
          God told the snake
                    to tell her to eat
And the only way we can live after we die
          and be young forever is
                    if we believe everything his Son
          that God sent here to be murdered
                    said.

Before I Can Fly and Sing

Ornithologists discovered
          each baby robin in the nest requires
                    14 feet of earthworms a day
          to survive
So if there are 6 baby robins in the nest
          it means 84 feet of earthworms a day
                    are required
          and figuring
Each earthworm is 4 inches
          give or take an inch
                    that means each baby robin needs
          42 earthworms a day.
Hmmm.... .and when you learn
          earthworm experts discovered
                    each worm has 10 hearts
          and is both male and female
That means each baby robin consumes
          420 earthworm hearts a day
                    and 42 times the earthworm know-how
          how to be both male and female.

Hmmm.... .no wonder
       robin song
            is so
      heartful!
How many worms
      do I need to eat
            every day
      before I can fly and sing?

Kite Flying Wisconsin

Flying a kite
      the shape of Wisconsin
            in Wisconsin—
Perfect replica of Wisconsin in miniature
      with all its cities and towns,
            all its rivers and lakes,
      all its forests and farms—
Seeing it soar up and up
      smaller and smaller
            till just a dot in the blue
      tugging the end of my line.
Up there almost lost from sight
      amid clouds and hovering hawks
            is Milwaukee where I live
      and Northwoods' haunts I love—
Is no one else in my state
      flying their state
            in kite shape
      high above
Thinking Wisconsin sails through space
      as much as the kite
            shaped like Wisconsin does
For the Earth is a kite the Sun flies
      and gravity
            its invisible string?
Should I let go? No,
      reel it in
            like a fish,
Wisconsin, come down from the sky!
      with all your cities and towns,
            all your rivers and lakes,
      all your forests and farms,

Closer, closer, Wisconsin-
Till I hold you in my arms again.

First Breath Last Breath

When a baby boy is born
      and the midwife
            holds him up
     as he takes
         his first breath,
Place him over
     the Mother's face
         so when the baby exhales
     his first breath on Earth
         the Mother breathes it.

And when the Mother dies,
     her middle-aged son
         the baby grew up to be –
     by her side,
         his head next to her head –
Follows her breathing with his breath
     as it becomes shorter,
         and as the dying Mother
     exhales her last breath
         her son inhales it.

First appeared in *The Sun*.

GUY BEINING

A Rueful Fit

5.
Hell is a
spot
between all else.
there, in the
yard
a chicken scratches
its comb.

30.
can we go anywhere
but here,
i mean that i
feel everything
has been sawed off.
& yet the endless
growth
goes in every direction.
there must be harmony
in the gravel
outside.

31.
hand to elbow;
arm thru a bandaged
Hell.
red oxen move the
pith from peach.
the oval wall
moves no one.
there is a silver clock
full of spoons
that bargains
for minutes.

37.
alotted,
the poor manner
of being,

in rice field,
swept up by a
mountain of Kings.

38.
i spent
the whole day
listening to myself
say nothing.
we are unprepared
to place the right
p e b b l e s
in our mouths.

39.
whatever you think,
as another thought jingles,
it is then
that the spearmint
sky
meets the chin.

40.
the window is
locked in the head;
island of it is
submerged in greenery.
how much fakeness is
painted out of one?
the air hears
a pin drop.

41.
a large swamp
of a cold,
wet day
passes thru me.
brushes brown cycles,
brooding.
can i go anywhere
with a holster
& no gun?

nothing chosen

the climate of the day
is not to be found
the rub of it stuck
between ice pick & lance,
between memory & threads
of material anger.
this day lays flat,
fighting syllable of mud
& chorus in mirror factory.

poised

hinged to outer view,
dropping bruises onto singed landscape,
leaving pencilled brows,
& lining up jars of facial creams.
somewhere there, to slip
tongue onto petal of light.
thought process grows as if
a bee zipping into a golden pocket,
as blue typewriter of the mind
tries to push a line.
the same question is fractured
into factions of a guess.

nuzzle 4.

M	oral	E
a		g
n		y
t		p
A	mule	T

on grid of war another divide
is scratched out along the tigris.
a mule in the form of a camel
had escaped egypt & the dessert, arriving
in the oral shriek of iraq,

feeling twisted hoods turn,
& finding an odd figure wearing
a manta & amulet
waiting for a new morale to
climb plexus of pyramid,
having riddled coin & eye of bill.
along the way an ant
spied the gyp of current politics
& disappeared into upturned columns.

the holy dream

i am on Christian hill,
or another hill of salt & shadows,
nowhere here to tame a dove,
or go the lines of a hymn,
the vortex being of principal cities dead,
anticipating nothing but precipitation from my head,

stir again some high wire act,
& close the pages of brush fires,
making the ball of us as kings,
in trappers view of cutting legs,
for we know the dirt in us
will feign a spell of bleeding,
tho the mirror will not find you there,
for it too has taken apart clouds in exodus.

last heard myself speak in a dream

anywhere i go
into the strange house
i see my past,
& view golden mirrors
tipping into the bare feet
of russia.
(you got to take this
from your head,
even tho it is the pillow
that blows the dream away.)
i don't know where

the gates are,
or the property that chips
the sky of a painting.

sentence of sound

chirp, chirp, a bird hatched
sound from its beak.
such a dreary hollowness,
not that the air could recall with certainty
it taps the moon twice on windowpane.
down the street a doorman
with a whistle strains the air.
to-me-i, spared all trails
leading to her face.
a beautifully wan look
that stills the flush of nature,
she being that poetic beam
with a garden full of expressions,
always able to trigger a thought.
no couplet or haiku can break her brow.
so went, the bird, the whistle,
& her voice in me.

ALAN CATLIN

Vertigo (2)
after Cindy Kelly

*"This high up, I begin to see how small our human realm is, face distances
and know the kingdom of perception is pure emptiness"*
          Po-Chu-I, "On Ling-Ying Tower, Looking North"

Seeing is everything
snow drifts are glazed in thin ice
are those dreamed of beasts
whose existence has never been conceded
except on certain clear nights

The moon is an allusion
a co-conspirator

conjoined at the hip of sight

All the furious internal tides
are unleashed as perfect storms
cranial fevers that shed weathered systems
as powdered rock

choking dust storms
dust devils that ape typhoon

water spouts
that funnel spume on all the blooded
acres sight has transformed
into a hunter's blind

a confusion of perceptions
becomes informed light
sickled in the field of vision
as chaff

as a mirage of false horizons

This far up
I begin to see how small our human realm is

Blood of the Poet

> *"Every poem is a coat of arms,*
> *it must be deciphered."*

The hands of the artist have
a life of their own as do all
the enchanted eyes, disembodied,
what they see a shadow reflected
in broken glass or hidden by
garments worn as cloaks around
the unmoving hands that control
a complete stoppage of Time,
the governance of beauty trapped
in an hour glass siphoned as wet
sand into a pit laced webs are
stretched over creating a false
sensing of secureness a deceit

of spiders clings to, their dangling
bodies weaving a hypnotic spell
none who entered here could
escape unaffected, not even the magus
freed at last from his confining
shell, his futile gestures made trying
to separate hidden gold from lead,
diamond minds from detached heads,
the secret of phlogiston safe from
unconscious minds, minds caught in
a shadow play of life that captures all
who stay, obsessed with the struggle
between life and death where all
questions must be referred, remain
unanswered, especially those queries
posed by poets who know less than
nothing about larger issues of metal
and man, man and Immortality, that
mortal tedium that can not be avoided,
not even by versifiers about whom it
has been said, "Poets - - shed not the red
blood of their hearts but the white blood
of their souls" and what good is that to us?

Self Portrait with False Prophet

"I have a good ear for wings"
Stan Rice

The mottled skin stretched tight over
carved statue in wood, part-canine, part
long-haired simian, sits staring in self-
hypnotic trance at nothing in this world,
long branch-like arms clutching at rose
petals, cane stems no longer bearing
passion fruits used as barter for strangers
looking for solutions to puzzles only
oracles can supply. The plush flowering
of unnatural hybrids are the staple growth
of mystic gardens the prophet uses for
daytime dozing and night times of autonomic
dreaming.   In this recklessness of sleep,
the paper wings of harpy birds bear the flame
of perpetual light. Though brightness

illuminates, what is seen cannot be transcribed
into something recognizable to the human mind.
The sanctuary forest that surrounds restless
spirits are facsimile versions of what he knows;
when it is time to speak, there are no words.

"Sometimes I just fall into it"

Maybe it was the year, Winter of '69,
'70, four feet of frozen snow every-
where, Arctic winds blasting over open
fields, the lights from Utica State
beckoning across that vast, white
expanse, maybe it was that useless
war I was eligible for, ready or not;
no prospects, nowhere to go, warm
flat beer in styrofoam cup, two joints
of Mexican in my brain, a Sneaky
Pete pint in my back pocket, half-gone
and after that? After that, more staring
at the lights, sitting, as I was cross-legged
in far corner of game-room-by-day-
pub-by-night place, adamantly alone, depressed
and dreaming of how depressing it would
be not to be depressed, my friends blowing
me off, realising it was useless to try and
rouse me from where I went without them,
not knowing I was seriously thinking of
never coming back and she said,
"I've never seen anyone as alone as you are."
And, I wondered who she might be and
why she might care, "I used to be that alone too.
And then I killed myself. In another life.
I'm back now for you." She said, holding out
her hand for me and I take it, allowing myself
to be guided into the night. As I go,
I can hear my friends laughing, loudly
talking among themselves, saying stuff
like, "Way to go." and "Strangest way I
ever saw to pick up a woman but if it works,
what the fuck." All those things they were
saying, as if I might be coming back.

An Explanation Provided for Localized Phenomena

The Rainbow Bridge is made
with I-Beams of light, also
know as eye-beams. What is
seen as spectral coloring and what
is not seen but known to be
ever-present is called extra-sensory
meaning colors we cannot but sense
are present in our minds. Twin arches
on the bridge are the main supports and
are commonly referred to as double
rainbows. Power generated by the falling
water and white rapids that occur in
the shape of a horseshoe are known as
water wheels. These water wheels
supply the energy that makes the cities
on both sides of the river glow in the dark.
Engineers refer to this miracle of eye-
beaming sight as night lighting.
Communities for miles around marvel
at these constructions and the light they
give off. The whirlpool that occurs when
dual currents meet are not waterfalls nor
twin arch related hence are known to be
a figment of the imagination.
When the rainbows fade, the bridge may
disappear. This may happen at night as well.

Portrait of the Artist with Four Naked Dancers

inside the Crazy Horse Saloon,
Paris after dark, a water colored
shade drawn for their shadows
to interact on, the artist fixed as
an ornamental statue allowing
their fawning, soulless caressing,
his one, good eye fixed on the smoke
inside bell jars resting on each café
table, the other, untrue one, outcast,
subject to the whims of green fairies

in slim glasses. A jazzband's discordant
hum summons spirits from a burnt
hearth, the fake Roman pillars on
either side of the bandstand, paint
chipped and worn where the waiters
have been chained, chaffing at their
bonds; their cork lined bar trays empty,
all the once-filled broken glasses
beneath their bleeding bare feet.

100 Women and an Octopus

The green haired ones and the blue,
the tiger-striped and platinum dyed,
those with shag wigs and 'Fros
encircled by sinuous limbs, enrapturing
arms opening portals, wounds, carapace,
in public places: Starbuck's tables,
plush club booths, on bar stools,
gallery spaces, lofts, special exhibitions,
unrivaled, incomparable, incomprehensible;
in private: what happens in bordellos,
country clubs, cat houses, nude revue
shows and private viewing booths:
the unbelievable, the unimaginable,
the unseemly, whatever money can
buy, the artist records.

DAVID CHORLTON

Van Goyen

Two oak trees rise from a world more air
than land, and more shadow
than light, against the portent of a storm
that has begun to darken the shoreline.

A gull makes a highlight against a universe
of mysteries and the thoughts
sent into it by men who gaze toward it

with their hands in their pockets, passing time
until the first thunderclap disturbs
the conversation they are having,

something no doubt about the taste of the wind
sailing from the north
with a cargo of salt and new hardships.

Night Calls

With a kiss of darkness comes the moth
cloaked in dust to the light
of a lamp by the latch on the door.
We sleep in uncharted territory

each night with our borders open
and waiting for messages
from creatures with whom we share
the floating world to enter

our dreams. When the unexpected
owl in the tree at the window
calls, the notes glow against the silence
and line our ears with threads and small bones.

Postcard from Bologna

with thanks to Tom

A postcard arrives from the province of Morandi
whose borders are the walls
of the room with a population of one
and whose army consists of bottles
standing to attention in coats of grey paint
applied by the man who directs item.

He invents a horizon, places an arrangement
before it, and dresses his imagination
in camouflage. Morandi is the minister
of interior space, discipline,
defence, and modesty. His daily routine
is to declare peace by wrapping

simple objects in light from a bulb
that hangs on a cord
from the sun at the centre of his ceiling.

Mockingbird

A mockingbird, at 2 AM, is singing
in the orange tree. The stars
make him do it, and the scent
in the blossoms that have opened around him.
He is the soundtrack
to a dream from which I have awoken
In which animals have entered
the city while we sleep:
the fox in his coat of fire, the lion
whose breath is silver light, and the jaguar
returned to reclaim their world.
I stumble to the song
running through the open window
and watch the lost coyote
playing with his shadow by the street lamp.

Photographic Memory

The inefficient eye of the cheapest camera
we could buy after our good one
went blind in the humidity
recorded what it could of the silver light
that shone in rain; hills unrolling
beneath clouds as they cleared;
chiaroscuro forest interiors, twisted barks
of trees drilling into the sky;
friends wading the river where a bridge
had washed away; the warm mist
that swallowed us and slowly dripping
palm fronds as they grew their sharpness back
when it cleared; ourselves
with heads cocked to examine sounds
that hopped from leaf to leaf;
a view along the fruit stalls on a street
yawning early in the day; waves too muscular

for sailing on; a bamboo seat
in a room without walls and the cross-hatched
foliage behind it where the collared aracari
briefly landed and turned to display
on its back a red so bright it was memory
even in the moment
it appeared.

KIRBY CONGDON

Rover

Tourists view the wonders seen
from town to town,
parade the casual leisure of their lives
in festivities of foreign ways,
behold the monuments
ancestors occupy,
tramp the battlefields that document
the wars they wage,
stroll along the bucolic picnic ground
where flags or fireworks celebrate
how forgotten heroes died.
Greedy eyes seize souvenirs
to prove a place, scanned, was there
as a transient, bored, passes on
to other news.
Shopkeepers sweep streets clean.
The debris of nameless feet is gone.
So, what hope can we suggest
beyond the halos of the moon?
What future lies in all our stars?
Is there any form of life
in the hard dust left
from the ancient tears dried up
on that far rock our machine,
eager, reaches for
on the barren plain of Mars?

The Anatomy Chart

By ancient arrangements the body's innards
in regulation work with all their clocks
like wind-up toys whose gears can't stop
and, wireless, are unattached,
to any source of time or thought
sensing only their torso's body-pain
and never know the worlds gone by
if both the eyes of their busy brain
close down when, spent,
a day-dream's life, dwindling, ends.
As the body-knowledge we extend
depends upon the thought of self
to define its own ideas of identity
and the organs of our sight beyond the mind
explore, like lost microscopes, our outer space
in galaxies to map the charts
to identify each universe we make
that faith or fiction dare create,
what we have at hand, we claim
by touch, hold in name, then, at last,
beyond the Big Bang's start, timeless, let go.
Intelligence celebrates in wonder
the unreal facts we find, verify and date
but which no mind's eye can, really, know
nor our brains' clever waves ever explicate.

Alarm Clock

Its life relies on winding up
the hard guts of those anxious works,
that factory hidden, shy, behind
the placid face of that flat facade
as it pleads with a tick, so alert!
answering with its tock in response
to prove to the world's room
time's press exists in the sixth sense
and sounds what believers hear:
I live, I live, I live
while the second-hand's unbending message
slices out our measured vision
by the blade of our precise decay,

giving trackless witness
to catastrophes struck relentless
in the fact of what's forever gone
and yet gives back with instant birth
creation's earth as time survives
in passing by and eats itself
as a casual cannibal behaves
whom no Bible nor prayer saves
when we wind up our universe
and keep time's order sane.

My finger joints
dance a compact ballet
which the wrist would twist and extend
to obey the mastermind
beyond the shoulder blade
when my whole body heeds
the power cast in the passing quirk
of some neuron's spark
sunk in silence there
in some sullen nodule of the brain's
ancient muddle of a somehow still exact design.
What generations of men laid down
the daily patterns of good sense
that lets this head behave by need,
if not by wish, as for some secret's deep desire,
or in long thought and finally, in my list,
for the foolish fantasy of a mind gone wild,
absorbed in ingenuity to engineer
the new beautiess found,
with the art of time, enlarged
in steeples, depots, kitchen shelves,
translating all our past to the present tense
as the flimsy proof of this existence
on which all our earnest hopes are built.

So wind the spring, reset the dials
that disasters, on occasion, interrupt.
Measure out the sun's decree
by which our hasty lives are, greedy, run,
Defy the madness habit brings
and heed the pulse the great machines,
in their astral seasons, though dead,
still give, and though lifeless,
can still provide

in that heartfelt drive that says,
I live. I live. I live.

Theorem

You have just, irretrieveably, lost ten seconds from the rest of your life when you should have spent it more wisely and profitably in the enhancement of your spirit and for the development of your psyche's well-being, as in reading a poem, listening to music or contemplating the stars, or better yet, in writing or composing or searching for those deep meanings in the menage of the universe for it is then, when we are most involved in work, that labor is easy.

When our attention is most keen on the details of perfection our study is light. When our concentration is most devout, time is quick. It is then we are most alive and escape the lie of mortality because the minutes fly through all the calendars and we can look up and see on all the birthdays the spinning centuries go by! But in the boredom of the watched pot, only death lives and it is we who die as time, arrested, stands still and the end of everything arrives. Eternity boils in the flames of the gourmet's consumption. Eat the meal the chef has laid before you or, by extinctions, be eaten.

Winter Burial
for Roseanne Ritzema

Funeral flowers from florists
flourish in careful arrangements
on coffins for celebrations
that life let us know
with blooms of tropical fires
burning, erotic
in the white dusting
of indifferent snow.
Our cold bodies unbend, to go on back,
reluctant, returning home
to shovel the bone-heaps left
of an old blizzard's gray debris
where, even so, crocuses, still,
remembering, may forgive regrets
and, ever eager, grow!

The Cyclotron

Our cyclotron discovered a way to make a miniature black hole, but, as you know, the administration advised against it. So we kept it quiet and worked on the project on our own time. We need to pursue knowledge for the sake of science. We need to pursue expertise for the sake of political advantage in a world of instability.

It was Sunday afternoon and we agreed we had found the theorem, the final equation that pulled all our research together. It was tiny and extremely complex, but the experiment worked. We had created an example of a black hole in the reactor. Through our microscope we saw it there, trembling a little as the light of our lamps showed neither a shadow nor a reflection. I took an dentist's pick to give that spot a little experimental poke. The tip of the metal rod I used disappeared. I let go of it in surprise and the handle slipped away without a trace.

An assistant was intrigued. He put a pencil he had in his hand at the same spot. The wood, the lead, the metal collar that held its eraser and the eraser itself melted away and, again, we saw no residue.

We looked at each other, not knowing whether we should congratulate ourselves on finding a secret of the universe, or try to figure out how to control it. But it was then we saw the laboratory lamp at our elbow lean to one side as the base of it began to turn into putty, became almost liquid and poured into the center of our observation table, just before its light went out.

"I'm going home!" our supervisor said.

I made a gesture questioning him, and indicated the building we were in, which had now gone dark.

"I have children," he replied, as if in answer. The foundation of the building had begun to creak.

Planes fly over the place now to investigate it but they don't come back. I try to explain why I left that city but they say I am upset. It's the war, they say. The President says he is going to address the country about all this very soon. Maybe even tomorrow.

DAVID COPE

After Lope

languid lines, mad thoughts
ripped from my rabid heart,
children of scorched eyes, speared ears,

heaved here enraged, unfree–
    abandoned, lost to the world,
so shattered & changed
you could only be known
thru the blood & come of your dreamsighs:
    since you've stolen the bullboy's labyrinth,
the waxwing dreamers' high flights,
the sea's fury, the flames of the abyss,
    if your serpentine dreams won't accept you,
leave the earth, dance in the winds
and rest in the eye of the storm.

Wild Calls in the Night

waking deep night strange wailing hiss & call some
weird bird below the hemlock-lined bank yet

close by– no agony in the wail, yet a talking call–
sex? or a manitou singer calling me spirits surely

awake in this wilderness rivergod rising to give me
her secrets in a language beyond my ken or guess–

& now, light rain & wind sweep up the valley, the
trees all hissing & turning above, patter-drops hitting

my tent where I muse & dream. Then silence– open
the flap & emerge to deer parading thru the clearing

now bounding thru brake pinestand & into swamp–
above, bright constellations never seen in city lights

turn in deep blue even as the river races by & owls
call from valley to valley: so I piss & greet the day.

Reagan RIP

ghosts attend him:
tens of thousands

thrown on the street
for a voodoo curve,

38

the slaughtered villagers
of El Salvador

he would've swept
from sight,

greasy smugglers
sent with arms to Iran–

down payment for
contra murderers,

AIDS victims
gone the dark way

once dismissed
as he danced

his imperial dance
for the cameras.

His Perfect Form

how he   slices
              thru waves arms slashing thru mirror
                        after mirror plunge & turn & glide
                                  up slice again–

in the showers,
              his lovely long calves & thighs,
                        small buns high up, hips grasped
                                  in dreams for thrust & sigh–

silken skin over
              six-pack tight & O what delight
                        must lie there, hands moving
                                  over soft flesh, that shy

smile over
              his shoulder, light above clouds,
                        tousled hair thrown back, wet streams
                                  flowing all down his perfect form–

Rush Hour in the Swamp, Near Hopewell Mounds

hard enough
                    with the rain dark flashing
                                    lane to lane,
                    no time to linger on men pulling
                                    up nets on
            the river beyond,
                            butts in mouth
                                    -fish flopping mad dancers
                            struggling with their deaths–

                                    no
                    time over here on the highway beyond
            sleepers in the mounds–
SUVs ram it right up your rear, racing
                    to their own deaths cellphones
                                    in their ears–
BLOWOUT–
                            cars skidding every way offroad

                    rolling metal lights flashing ending
            on their sides,
others askew
                    stopped dead above, stalled drivers
shrugging it off as a
            door pops open below
                                    & a face emerges in flashlights–
figures running in the dark– rain now
                            hammering roofs &
                    road & swamp alike.

Starlight Call

brothers & sisters
call back & forth
frantic–

she's confused she's
got piles of dirty laundry
can't remember what she

said when said who said &
now she's lost a whole day—
uncertain what happened

between dawn
when she was following
doctor's orders

(going to breakfast)
& the starlight call
when, strangely alert, she

remembers she should
have gone to
breakfast & can't figure

what passed
between dawn &
dusk—

& now
the brain scan,
the terminal

waiting.

Vita Nuova

for Alex & Carmen

coming here, they bore islands, peninsulas,
ledges, sunflowers & rosemary, quick songs,
& neither knew nor saw they'd raise their palms

to find each other. the way was rock-strewn,
thorny, blindly turning in the hollow echoes
of memory & the quick sighs of desire.

tonight—lovers—they breathe together in
a timeless *now* by the moonlit river flashing
its thousand lights as the final gypsy violin

slides from evening lament to quiet
paean & switchback to silence where
their touch springs streams from

the dry rock & they find ways up thru
wild dreams into rainforming rare air,
breath that words new life to love.

Ghazal of the Singing Shadow

thru the swamp mottled green & yellow shadeshine cool
        September morning you turn
as does leap high thru brush into scrub woods low hills beyond
        muck pools & eddies

the river racing fast after rains all sign of drought gone in the
        flashing water. the crisp air
belies stalled traffic in Texas Rita boiling the Gulf into a rage of
        wind & rain lake waters

already flooding thru patched levees newly freed streets & homes
        suddenly aflood again.
she had journeyed south only weeks before to bury her mom,
        dead awaiting heart surgery

in a small town hospital as Katrina roared ashore. streets she'd
        walked in charged memories
of childhood now were tunnels of wreckage downed lines piled
        garbage dead animals

yet strangely they found the lost deacon who could OK the burial,
        the greens for the casket,
the pot of red beans & rice for the wake & even gas to get there &
        back through test after

test of patience. the journey thru such sorrow melds to songs in
        moonlight where your
shadow follows you as in day, where you become the shade
        walking beside yourself looking

back thru you & the shadow world becomes a world of light
        where memory's lovers turn
& pass thru your very bones & eyes in the white silence of the
        moon & the warm hands

42

clasped together in a wilderness of thoughts. here too the stars
        turn in their heavenly courses
unseen by the attentive eye, though the earth is solid & the
        breathing calm. when the ashes

that once were man swirl in the turning current & the lovers
        stand on the shore sighing
at the life they've left, his grey eyes wild heart strong back &
        dancing song, finally then,

the dawn comes & you find your way back thru that turning
        morning to the leaping does
& the solitary heron arrowing upriver like a blue streak over
        endless shining waves.

JOHN ELSBERG

The Zen Of Rowing

Steering a straight line.
The secret is in the motion,
not in strength.

On Saturday she smiled
as the ripples flowed
from her hand. I want to lose

ten pounds this summer. If only
I could lose it this way,
rowing, with her smiling at me,

smiling, or even not smiling.

Questions

Tell me, is a rose really naked
or is it her very own dress?
                    Pablo Neruda

Tell me, is the snow really quiet
or is it its own way of calling?

Tell me, do all shadows need light
or do some bring their own?

Tell me, is she ever truly alone
or are we all her very own song?

Riff On Rimbaud
for Eric Greinke

1.
blue coffin
blonde waterfall
red scratches of dawn

black water
beneath a fading starless night
bold trees

rose tattoo
its prickly flicker on my lips
    beeing

big black wheels   this winter's all about demons

2.
rope bridge
tangled between bat wings
vestal storm

all this
suspended above my heart
the pallor is mine

44

fine-tuning
the edge of the loony sea
   tiny shovels

angels shorn with the sheep   vast eyes of the hills

JEAN ESTEVE

Undubbed

I dub your mind the octopus
        of politics, the way its tentacles
explore between the rocks
        of our embodiments
to prod our sorry, shadowy desires.

It's time to laugh. We all know now
        the little nut of your procedural
probes at our unmentionables
        nestles in your own
ruttish, most seditious scurvy part.

I undub you. The octopus,
        biologists find to be intelligent,
eloquent their ink and
        so singular their prospect
as would never deign to model as facsimile
        of janitor-in-chief gone daft.

Different as Night and Day

Daytime is a TV screen
where all we hope to be
is what the someone elses mean
for us to feel and see,

but nighttime still belongs to us,
its homely anarchy
all a-fuck with lust and chaos,
tenderness and glory.

Demonstration

I'm here to demonstrate
how to strate the demons
from the belly
they invaded
the moment you were born.

Take two lovely lemons
and strate them evenly
along the axis
of your grimace.
Now that devil is forsworn.

Healthy

Me? I'm healthy as a horse.
Just visiting,
performing my daily good-work.

So when that shadowless nurse
starched in, you bet I grabbed my purse,
throwing back over my shoulder a
hurried "I'll phone ya."

Notebook: still-life

Sprawled across sun squares
she stares out the window
waiting for September storms
to flush her of summer.

Busy

You'll have to wait. I have to eat,
then trim my nails and clean my teeth,
and bathe, then find a place to stow
leftover food and dirty clothes.

Wait. I want to catch my breath.
Impossible. I haven't yet
filled up enough of this grim day
to keep the wolf of memory at bay.

Your Flower

If she is your flower
firm and ferocious
snarling at winds that tousle and bend her

           you be her tender

easily kneeling
your tender hands tamping the ground

           and surround her

with romantic fingers your pokers and probes
caressing the smooth brave stem

           the swelling of bulb

and pluck her
as fancy demands.

No Valentine

Like a thief, I wormed my way
        into your office,
crawled inside your file drawers,
        checked out "J" for Jeanie.

I should have guessed the skinny folder
        held only an E mail list
of puns, some funny-papers, a recipe
        for boiled potatoes, but no valentine, no porn.

Bless me, Father, I have sinned
        when like a worm I thieved
his potted tree of tangerines,
        so cankered, I, by fury.

Obedience

What he wants me to be is good
which is why he lays a table for me heavy with sex and food,
chocolate, caramel, butterscotch, popcorn, whiskey
and himself. I undo buttons, set about my duties briskly.

MICHAEL FLANAGAN

always the chance

to wade into the
ocean, farther and
farther, deep water
high waves until
you are too far,
to step off a
bridge, a roof-
top, in front of
a train, there's
always the chance
of a change of
heart, those
seconds, that
fear, suddenly
knowing you would
step back given
the chance, arms
flailing, swimming
wildly, grasping
for what moments
ago you'd scorned,
or found too hard,
always the chance
there will be no
more tomorrow, just
when you've decided
you don't really
want things to end

without reason

the air over
the side-
walk, cold
wind, alley-
ways with
iron fire
escapes, a
night in the
month of
November,
a late hour,
slow moving,
hands in your
pockets, streets
wet from some
early rain, the
sound of dis-
tant traffic, a
single deep
breath, and
without reason,
suddenly, you
feel more alive
than you ever
have before

you slide

the old sins creep like
dengue fever, they crawl
the staircase to grip your
hand, your hand shakes
with fear and love, your
knees bend toward some
lost calling, the wasted
years scream remember,
you look away, without
thought or hesitation,
you beg a small favor,
a dose of willful blind-
ness, in the morning,

before you are fully
awake, mortality
stands on your throat,
the weight of its in-
difference the worst of
all, you pity yourself,
you dream better yet
the days are a ruin,
the real air you wish to
own coughs, it staggers
out of the corner and
dies, you are unable
to march to the beat of
bright angles, a gray
tundra, you slide

nocturnal

i like the dead weight
of the world when I
look out my window,
i like a lone car some
where in the distance,
so in the black ink
of late evening you
can really hear the
tires on the road,
i like to wander
down my driveway,
stop at the curb and
look down the street
at the absence of
people, on a good
night black gray
clouds moving
fast across a gray
blue moon, the
wind pulling things
around, the hint of
unusual moments,
loud in the silence
of every sound

HUGH FOX

from Time - A Life Cycle

II.
Watching a video tape interview with
A.D. Winans in San Francisco, Vesuvio's
restaurant, eight years ago, he looked old
even then, Richard Morris in the corner,
watching, the camera strays to him once in
a while, looking haggard and frail, dead maybe
three years already, I oughta say *Everyone's*
gotta die, why not just get used to the idea
(Anne Bancroft dead today, 73, exactly my
age), only what I want is a forever of fried
onions, candied pineapple, soft beds,
Bernadete's ears and eyes, listening, lilacs
and clematis, my kids and their pals and their
own growing, multiplying Foreverness.

III.
Never should have watched the video of Bernadete
and me in Paris about twelve years ago, Chris twelve,
the street musicians, guitars, a little keyboard, drums,
selling chickens and roosters in cages on the sidewalks
just next to the Seine, a carnivalesque sense of hooligan
good-times, let it flow the way it flows, even the pyramid
at the Louvre, city as party, life as Do It The Way You Want,
drum as you drum, go as you go, come as you come.

IV.
Dangerous to keep watching the old videos, Brazil,
then Scotland, another trip to Paris, the kids growing
up in Michigan, Kansas City, all the different houses
over the years, Bernadete's black nylon legs on our
wedding night, me playing one of my etudes on a piano
over in the music building at the university, so much
flowing, Irish Creme, life as delicatessen, for a moment
I think of Hemingway, D.A. Levy, why not just end it
while the deliciousness is still flowing?

IX.
Flowing into the hills now, the wheat
goldening, even the idiot-corn thigh-high,
becoming the Earth, meteorites carving
out the oceans, the growing-dying moon,
eternal trees, liquifying, everything
becoming gas, light, cyclically dying and
forever (cyclically) reborn.

X.
"What's the difference, you 'make it' or
you don't 'make it,' you can see the Manhattan
or Kansas City or Minneapolis skyline or not,
you're CEO or CFO or Chief Nobody, she's got
great legs, she makes great double-chocolate cakes,
you've got a Mercedes and...you know what I
mean," he starts to cry, his Scotch beauty, 5'10"
blonde snowball 'nurse'/'caretaker' puts her
arms around his shoulders, "Maybe that's enough
visiting for the day, deary..," shooing me to go, I
give him a little hug, "Until....," out into the misty,
drizzly dusk, 90 degrees yesterday, 59 today, if it
snowed, I wouldn't be surprised.

XI.
The day you never wanted to arrive, arrives, the parks
full of kids, all the mothers out, legs and arms, hair, kid-
scream laugh noise, the birds crazy in the bushes and trees,
Hungarian perfect legs out jogging, ass screaming NOW,
NOW, NOW, quesadillas and sour cream for lunch, red
cherries and black currants, grey tumor clouds and sun-sun-sun
until the 60% full-moon comes out over the barely moving
river, a few words with all three wives, four of my kids,
the swollen ankles still swollen, some kind of heart Ecco
test scheduled for next week by my 24-hour-a-day M.D.
present wife.

Class Struggle

Inner/outer cities, big cash, big smash,
Leoncavallo's Party Store, Bud Lite,
Cabernet Sauvignon, FOR SALE signs
in all the wrong/almost-wrong neighborhoods,

who's gonna have a dollar for Made in China
dollar stores, but we still find Louis XIV-ish mansions
overlooking magic river-scenes, eighty dollar shirts,
garage sale me, 25 cent ties, I buy the whole
schmear.

Prophets
for Richard Krech

Poison-ivy growing up the side of a windmill
gloriously ketchup red, the corn all dried out,
cows, why always the goats now in the fields
with them, are they cow-farmers, heavy mists
across the sinking sun turning it into a red balloon,
chance so artistic and (acorns, chestnuts, flame-red
maples) so clever, designer-design, I pass an old
Adventist church on a dirt road to nowhere, want
to buy the old farmhouse down the road a few feet,
go in and wait for the Christ, redemption, eternal
beatific-visioned heaven, not just a guillotining
into nothingness.

Where The Deer And The Antelope Roam

Down Upton to Cutler, dirt road, down half a
block road into the forest, palace after palace,
Deer Run Lane, we see four deer that disappear
into the forest, pines and oaks, maples, catalpa,
coneflowers and Queen Anne's Lace, marshgrass,
cat-tails, ducks, "The biggest mistake was to create
ONE God or a trinity, whatever, can't you feel the
cone-flower gods, the cat-tail goddesses, duck-gods,
pine-goddesses...I'd be happy out here in just a
shack," turning to her for a nod, confirmation,
acknowledgement, one of the castles for sale, but
she's asleep...the usual, like every night when we watch
the weather or the local news, just before we go to bed.

53

Walking Around

Walking around in the winter city streets, more nose than anything else, smelling the sauerkraut and sausages, lard, lentils, sauerkraut soup, dumpling and I'm in Grandma Prague again, the only sanity I ever had, except, ah, Tapas, artichokes, chorizo sausage, egg-quarters, and Valencia says *"Bienvenido de nuevo a tu España*/ Welcome back to your Spain," with an accent on the your, another street down and Lucia's Ceviche de Pescado is whitefishing through the garlic-lime winter air, "Why did you ever leave me?," wanting to say "I didn't...," or an eternal "I'm back....," night carrying me into the warehouse district still being converted into condominiums and restaurants, on my way to I know not where.

Thou Shalt

Thou shalt plant corn and mint, calabashes
and cabbage, guava and avocados, datura
and coca, baby-carriage thy babies late afternoons
down the shadiest streets possible, drink your malt
beer at dinner, swim in the pools, seas, rivers
and lagoons, pray to the trees and stars, pay
homage to the clouds and hills, divinize the
deer and moles, couple thy eggs and sperm,
pray to the dark and the daily newborn sun,
drown all thy Thou Shalt Nots in a serene sea of
Satori.

Here

The cats asleep on the bed and the top of the
cat-perch, the water flouncing in the fountain
outside, wind through the lilacs and palms,
the distant farting of a jet, gone in seconds, a few
sharp stabs in my (left side) chest, then gone,
fifteen minutes, *Ça sufit*/ that's enough, finger-
examine my chest, find the rib-sternum articulation
where the pain is, outside in the garden for lunch,
I wanna be a cat slinking along rubbing my flanks against
chairs, sniffing the grass, rubbing my head on
the bottom of one of the chairs, staring at
Monique and Jim, rubbing, staring, getting

interested in the salami, eyes, touch, smell, the
sanity of HERE, HERE, HERE.

The Buddha

The Buddha-day finally comes, I count twelve different pushing-to-their-
limits birdsongs, the new-green backyard flooded with rain and snow-melt,
Gettysburg and all the rest vanish, "It happens to me five or six times a day,
like I've been cut in half and my lower half falls to the ground, another
week, month, year...," sleeping pills, arthritis pills, anti a-to-z pills, new ivy
all over our concrete block walls, invading the back windows as the sun
goes down she comes out with dishes of guava mixed with praline ice cream
and the first bat I've seen for months, noiselessly takes flight across the
emerging moon.

ERIC GREINKE

For The Living Dead

1.
I rise with an effort
I feel the dead
They vibrate
In my foggy heart
Like icebergs colliding
In oceans of blood

I am alone
I sit by my window
I become a stone
Like stagnant water
Or steady drumming
I was once a prisoner too

I hear again
The familiar beat
Inside my heart
The divine rhythm
Of the countless dead
The rainstorms of light

2.
The zombies are revolting
They are crude in their culinary habits
Eating the flesh of the living
Raw with no seasoning
Duly elected representatives
With secret term limits

Sound the alarm
The flesh-eaters are in the house
They are slow but they keep on coming
They are mesmerized by fireworks
They like to run amok
When they aren't milling aimlessly

Zombies have no sex lives
They share the despair of the wolfman
Drunk on power under the full moon
Soaked in gasoline waiting for a light
Enflamed by love & hate
Counting down to the final insult

3.
A cipher falls dead in the snow
From a bus of discontinued androids
Last year's models obsolete versions
Of absolute ideals polished
To insane shines that reflect
The light that cannot be silenced

Jolly gunshots wound our pride
Armies of pleasure reap
Rewards of perfect cartoon murders
Buddhas smithereened by friendly fire
Floating in rivers of polite bodies
Joyfully waving their black flags

They are the human furniture
They are the living dishrags
They are the constant reminders
They are the ruined fortresses
Engorged on cloned flesh
Fitted with artificial hearts

4.
In the post-apocalyptic world
The zombies are loosely organized
With no zombie leader
They wander in random abandon
Trying to play various musical instruments
But their rhythm is shot

A small group of human survivors
Still comb their hair & wear make-up
Drooling & shuffling their feet
The zombies are mystified
By the smallest most subtle stimuli
But their haunted bony faces never smile

In the land of the dead
If a zombie bites you
You become a zombie too
You become a soldier in the zombie army
Sharing a goal with no sense of purpose
With an inner drive to obey

5.
The red bird still sings
In the green earth tree
In the airtight shopping mall
In the fenced-off arena
In shadows of tall buildings
In shacks of toothpicks

Robots built by zombies
Then put in charge
The doors are all locked
Impervious to your meat cleavers
Oblivious to your howls of pain
Ungrateful for your sacrifices

We navigate by dead reckoning
Our options are greatly reduced
We search in vain for a way out
Disguised by decadent cosmetics
The sentries at the gate are drunk
When the invasion comes they will die

6.
What can we do
What do we know
We who are barely human
We who have broken the 7th seal
We who have left the gate open
We who have stolen the Golden Fleece

Now the ghosts swallow us
We sullenly celebrate their loss
Our eyes opened wide as greed
Our diamonds soaked in blood
The coldest heads prevail
To organize the slaughter

Where have we been
What have we done
We mounted the final burial mound
We heard again the ancient last rites
We cloned sheep by the herd
We unleashed the living dead

7.
The robots are in formation
Speaking in unison
They all have the same face
Humorously humorless
They bow & scrape
Without relish or anguish

Robot malfunctions
Are inconvenient
Animated by artificial energy
Their movements are spooky
Unaware of planned obsolescence
Or constant surveillance

They make good household servants
They make good food service workers
They don't mind piece-work
Efficient & cost effective
Prison guards, they
Know no fear

8.
They don't need names
They don't have dreams
They don't throw temper tantrums
They're not ticklish
They don't itch much
They never need vacations

They don't get pregnant
They don't get drunk
They don't smoke
They don't eat or shit
They know not art
They hardly ever fart

A robot may be decommissioned
When a better model is developed
Many of the latest prototypes
Are biodegradable
They utilize virtual fibers
To simulate the naturally organic

9.
The severed head of Orpheus screams
Among the ashes of ancestors
Among the names carved into stone
In secret caves & hidden places
In tedious epics of doomed voyages
To the edge of the world

Organic life is prone to rot
Wooden puppets become brittle
Formaldehyde replaces blood
When the machine rules
Over the maker of machines
Which ones are the tools

Ghost lost before the body
Toy soldier left out in the rain
Hollow & impervious to pain
The pounding of robot feet
Grows louder by the parameter
Drowning out the earths heart

10.
I feel the spirits of the dead
They explode like seedpods
A thousand downy spheres
Doors that won't stay closed
Locks meant to be broken
Dandelions born in the wind

Beats of light drummed by spirits
Into the pulsating heart of sound
Into the unsanctified dirt
Out to the edges of space
Through the wounded waters
Beyond the toxic pain of time

I hear the call of light
Through the mechanical darkness
Through the marching shadows
Through the neutral rocks
The stale bread that feeds
The dreams of the anemic world

First appeared in *Wilderness House Literary Review*.

The Mist
for Glenna Luschei

I wander
Through memory caverns
In search
Of the elusive present,
Like a big fish
That struggles upstream
To spawn in times river
One last time.

Like a mad wind
In an ancient storm,
Dead friends
Pierce the peaceful solitude
Where I have come
To take my soft rest
In the depth
Of a winter night's dream.

In the arid badlands
Of desire,
Past the long watches
Of sleepless nights,
I hold communion
With those lost ghosts,
Even as I pass into
The ever-darkening mist.

First appeared in *The Pedestal*.

JOHN GREY

Broken Pipe

Is it? Am I?
Depressed. Is that the right word?
And all because a pipe burst?

Wet, dry,
what's the difference?
If feelings aren't happening,
how can I diagnose?

No pain exactly.
Just these perceptions
that do some of the same things
pain does.
Ouch! That recrimination hurt.
Besides, this dark brown lake
is feeding off my toes.

I should see a doctor,
says one.
I'd prefer a plumber.
It's all in the mind,
says another.
Everything?
Even the nozzle
and the gasket?

Looks like another day
in which the massive ego massaging
will not be forthcoming.

For ego trampling
has replaced stomach gouging.
Misspent ardors
hurt like hell.
It's this floor I reckon.
There's been a lot of flooding.

One September

I lived in a cottage by a pond,
a summer place,
four small rooms, high rafters.
In the evening,
landscape left me,
surface fading into shore,
into the surrounding trees,
swallowing the grey-faced mountains.
What the one lamp couldn't shine upon,
became invisible.
The tapping of my fingers
was the only sound allowed.
The moon rose full, opaque,
along a corridor of stars.
Abandoned by the sun,
a lone coyote howled.
But I saw no moon.
I heard no coyote.

For, in a solitary chair,
blanket over my knees,
I drifted off.
A young woman came to me,
gold-haired, pink-cheeked,
more illustration from a book than real.
I did not know what to say to her.
Is it true if I speak it in a dream?
She seemed to recognize me,
came to me, held me close.
For the longest time,
she rose in my sky,
she howled in my head.

The Storm

Blow, blow, whoever you are that's the opposite of Gabriel.
Blow to your black heart's content.
There's a hellhound in the wind.
Wild nights! Gerard thought he saw
a rhinoceros rumbling through the town square.
He said, "I know I was wrong but it was true anyhow."
He went back to his dark one, his widow, was consoled
until the next loud clap of drum-skin clouds.
Henry's artwork fared better. The muse dropped down
on a streak of lightning. Her hair was singed but otherwise...
He painted the eel, the siren, the incinerated virgin.
Moira was playing who will die first, she or her cat.
That feline devil sat upon her lap, twisted its claws into her knees.
Moira blamed fright but such creatures are in league with storms.
The cat gripped the red eye of the weather and originated so much.
How black the temple veins of Boone.
He's counting the seven deadly on his fingers.
How many more would there be if it were the snake
and Eve who dwelt in Eden and Adam was the one
coiled up in the tree.
And then a limb snaps somewhere in the woods.
Adam topples, busts his skull.
The houses on this street aren't up to it.
Walls are thin as the bonds of thieves.
Roofs rattle. Candles flutter in flight and fear.
Nerve ends break like waves across Lady's trembling shore.
Thunder rumbles outside her window, like a great ship
inviting her to go sailing in dark, choppy seas.
Then rain comes pelting down, translates all that has come before.
Jacob is out in it without an umbrella.
And then an umbrella is seen skittering along the gutter,
without Jacob, so they think.

CAROL HAMILTON

Cadenza

I hold my breath
as you head off
to improvise your life.

The score rests
on the conductor's stand,
and even if we each
held a copy, our eyes
would rest in middle distance
as his do, none of us
able to focus on where
you are going,
none of us knowing.
I want you to circle back
in brilliant arcs,
but perhaps your leaps
and ecstasy will take
you clean and clear away,
and I here still,
right here for one more day.

Adaptation

The birds scavenge at the local landfills,
swoop and cry over the burning dump
at Matamoros, and in Spain,
they no longer migrate,
ensconced at the huge garbage
wasteland at Valdemingomez.
He says there the birds line
their Big Mac box nests
with unwound cassette tape,
raise their young in comfort,
flock to and stay with the easy life.
Some undetected people watcher
might note our cars swarming
through the fast food parking lots.
Some subtle shift in genes
may come in time, but meanwhile,
easy abundance tells us to settle in.
Like those to the California Gold Rush,
we choose our myriad get-rich chances,
flurry about for a chance to win
without much struggle,
and we are so pleased to live
in heaven, all too full of what
we do not need.

Taking Stock

Are we, as he said,
busy cataloging things,
or maybe we mainly
try to buy them
take them out of circulation,
shift their shelf lives,
switch the set up before
the equation sign. Some choose
not a battle to save the land
but a buy out. Nothing
in this world or out is safe
from our flag plantings.
I take inventory, but everything
on the list is named ME.

Almost Unbearable

The cold, she said,
a riff on pain
or where arrow enters,
another the dangled flesh
of dismemberment,
the chasm too deep and black
to swallow
when love is ripped off.

Today I'll pull up
the tomatoes
before the frost
desiccates those pushy, virile vines
that flowered yellow
everywhere
just days ago.
We're all brought low.

The Jerusalem artichokes
have fallen like trees
in the forest,
sap-stopped and top heavy.
The buried roots will nourish later
though light slips away

every, every single day
and I sit, ever
on the cusp of nothingness.

Once more Orpheus has begun
        his long climb
            to the surface
even as his shaky faith
        rides his back,
                    devours his trust,
    the one reason we must learn
        to lie.
        There on that aperture's rim
            wait I.

Tarantula

Childhood terror,
teenage church camp fear,
those cabins with creeping walls,
furry walls walking,
old jungle movies,
            the hero or heroine
oblivious, asleep, soon to be dervished,
my father's book with a picture,
            black and white,
and I accuse you now,
my brother's friend then,
            of chasing me with it.
Was it you?

In the real jungle,
I slept under net,
placed hands and feet carefully.
But West Texas campground,
            the bathhouse,
and a real one sat, like a werewolf s fist,
beside the trashcan.
            I made each entrance
and exit warily, skirted
the pavement where it waited,
            confused? sleeping? terrified?

66

It never moved.
I was as sorry as if it were
a fawn crushed beside the highway,
the sand crane crumpled,
wings angled and all poking at air,
falling to the hunter's will,
when I returned to find it smashed.

The two minds war
with the world as it is,
and I've yet to gain wisdom
from any life or death
        or safety ...courage, either.
I was sorry he was broken.
That was all.

Autumn Came While I Was Gone

No soft dampness now.
I return to brittle gold
and air cleared of all
except departure
and jittery leaves dancing
their crisp sweeps and turns
across yellow Pointillist fields
above and below, this all
seen against blue, blue sky.
I will welcome winter
when these showy summer guests
have left, finished with their flourishes
and their eager, excited goodbyes.

Faust's First Visit to Oklahoma

or was it? My first opera, with a cross-state trip to Tulsa, stars from the
Met and a local chorus waiting. The choristers had eager relatives dashing
forward to flash and hurry back to seat with photographic records of the
event, while one local sang loudly off key. Marguerita's spinning wheel fell
and rolled away. The gate to her garden stuck, so Faust had to jerk and pull
to enter and tempt her. Undeterred, I later went to "Pagliacci" and
"Cavalleria Rusticana" touring to Oklahoma City with Robert Merrill and
a full cast. A janitor entered out high balcony perch and tossed his keys in

a nervous tick as he listened with who knew what thought, until an enthusiast reached across me to rap him hard with his furled umbrella. My neighboring, dignified university professor started home between Acts I and II of the longer opera, returned, sheepish and better informed. We were eager in those days, but surely showed ourselves as cheery bumpkins to those traveling musicians. Yesterday I listened to "Faust" again and smiled. We still sometimes betray our prairie innocence, and we silently tap the uninitiated who bursts into applause after the first movement with our psychic umbrellas. We keep hoping that someday, some dull and well-tamed day, propriety will have overcome enthusiasm, even here on these impetuous plains.

DOUG HOLDER

I Saw Myself on the Dudley Bus That Day

I saw myself on the Dudley bus that day
his eyes: a blinking, flirt
with the mid-winter's sun-
watching
the slow, fade
of a dying afternoon,
his face shadowed
in five o'clock.
Half light,
no hair.
A bus of exiles
each mired
in their personal
affairs.

And that man
perhaps me
looked a million
miles away.
I believe I saw
him briefly yesterday,
and for a first time
on that day
we saw each other
and quickly
turned away

The Undertaker Takes His Lunch
Observed at the Sherman Café, Somerville, MA

The undertaker delicately wipes his mouth
another repast
has passed.
He scans the tabloid-
no need to note
the obits.
And in his seemingly flawless
black suit
I detect- -
perhaps a shadow,
nothing more
than a commonplace stain.

And that seam
seems...
Well,
a bit frayed
merely
a subtle...

yes, that's it

an innuendo
of wear.

The undertaker
runs his well-veined hand
through the shoe polish
in his hair - -

Just below,
his
gray roots grow

Looking at a Lone Woman at a Bar
inspired by a photo by Dianne Arbus

They are always
Impenetrable.

A dead stare
At the wall.

Her drink
Some half-empty
Prop.

Oh yes
The cigarette.
She holds a torch
But
For what?

No-
My gaze
Will not be
Met.
And
She will
Walk
Out the door.

And the clues
She will leave
The lipstick stain
On a crumpled
Cocktail napkin
The untouched
Nuts
A certain
Dead-end.

And the cigarette
Will smolder
And the smoke
Will wind
On its trail
To oblivion.

Jack's Joke Shop

Jack's Joke Shop was a mainstay in Boston. It recently closed its doors.

And you never forgot
Your first leering
Dick Nixon mask.

Your skinny college
Freshman body
Crowned with
That jaded
Face of hate
And Watergate.

And all that
Crass gas
Of the clandestine
Well-appointed
Whoopee cushion
That careened
From the unsuspecting
Ass of a maiden aunt.

How about that clock
Titled "No sex till six.?"
And its face
In an oh-so fortunate
Carnal circle of sixes.

And the prop
Of a knife
Through your smooth
Balding head
And your eyeballs,
Popping from
Your sockets
Riding on slinky springs.

And you a grown man
Laughing at a silly toy.

And you
Are still
That scrappy
Brat of a boy.
Periodical Room: Boston Public Library

Old man
Is their salvation
In that
Dog-eared
Edition of
The Anchorage Times?

You hold it
Like a loved one.
You read the front page
Like a face.
Your forehead kissed
With printer's ink.

The antiquated fan
Spins the old smells
Of the room
That your nostrils devour
Hungry for memories.

Does your mind drift
To the lost cities
Of your youth?
Are you outside of yourself?
Free from your bone-tired corpus
Answering some elusive call?

ROBERT K. JOHNSON

When Embattled

To know your mind consists
of a castle with parapets,
and that if part of the bulwark
cannot withstand the pressures

that besiege your days, you can always
rally your reasoning powers
and, sharp as a sword, repulse
your enemy
                    is to live

in a child's fairyland.
Your mind is no stalwart fortress
but a flag high on a pole
in an outpost, and someday

rampaging doubts and fears
you can't even imagine now
will rear up, primal and wild,
rip that flag to shreds
and hurl it into the darkness.

A Prediction

The moment before her face,
though ashen-white with sadness,
manages to turn away

from me, my taut lips whisper,
while all my skin is on fire,

"No one will ever love you
as much as I love you.,"

which she, too, knows will prove true.
But what I don't know yet

is that I will never again
see reflected in my mirror
the person who spoke those words.

Night School

In the hush of my room
I pause a moment
outside the haven
of the history book
I am reading,
and the stillness drops
its guise of benign,

silently whispers
"Watch - - you want

to learn - - watch"
and widens far
beyond the room,
the house, the town
stretches beyond

the puny earth,
surges into
a measureless darkness
while I - - too
terrified to tremble - -
cling to
my book's thin edge.

Uncertainty

Once, I shared
a first slow kiss
that, like a mountain peak
wind-cleared of fog,
revealed a world
wide as the dawn;

                 but later,
on a night
sadness made twice as dark,
I heard the one
I still loved
whisper a last goodbye

while I, like a pebble,
rolled, tumbled down
from that high peak,
became an avalanche
of pain that fell
for weeks, for months.

Can I ever come close
to what I felt
that first time,
             even though
my scarred body will resist
being coaxed to risk

another plunge
through night-dark pain
and even though that past
slow kiss emerged,
like a golden soundless song,
from a pure love.

To My Imagination

Heavy with fatigue,
I sit in a moonlit room
where you - - feeding on all
my many doubts and fears - -

dim the far wall's glow
pale as an old gravestone
and blacken the long shadows
that twist higher up my legs.

Yet at other times, when I - -
fresh from a sound sleep - -
gaze at the dawn beyond
my bedroom window, you turn

a branch's row of raindrops
into tiny silver birds
whose singing rings out like bells
amid the brightening air.

ARTHUR WINFIELD KNIGHT

Cesar Romero Plays The Slots

Cesar Romero, I swear I saw you
playing the slots at Casino West,
although I know you've been dead
for more than a decade now.
You were drinking a draft beer
bent over the poker machine,
feeding it quarters, oblivious

to everyone around you.
You had grey hair and a mustache,
and were dressed elegantly
for someone in rural Nevada,
for someone anywhere.
You ought to be in Vegas,
shaking hands with people
who loved your movies,
who called you the "Latin lover."
You portrayed Charlie Chan,
Doc Holliday and the Cisco Kid -
several times - but here you are
playing the slots. It's amazing.

Out West

Michael and I lean against
the adobe walls of the mission
on the square in Sonoma.
We're wearing cowboy hats
and Tony Lama boots.
The sunglasses are anachronistic.
Our dusters cover our shotguns.
The only thing is
we don't have any shotguns,
but mothers and frightened
children duck into doorways
when they see us. They know
we're bad hombres.

Letter To Richard In Sacramento

Kit always wanted to get up at 3 a.m.
and go down to the casino
to see who was there and what was happening
anytime we were in Nevada.
I always said, "Not much," but I was guessing.
She hasn't quit talking about 3 a.m.
since we moved here, so when I woke up
at 2:45 last night, instead of getting up
and going to the bathroom

and getting a glass of water, I said, "Let's go."
We put on some clothes, got into the car
and drove to Casino West. A cocktail waitress
was playing the slots and our favorite barmaid,
Maggie, was drinking a light beer
and talking to a cleaning lady. That was it.
Kit explored the place to make sure
no one was hiding, then she and I
had a glass of chardonnay, talked to Maggie,
and came home to our dog. Maybe
there would be some nightlife
in one of the high rolling places
in Vegas, but I got it right years ago.

The Outlaws

We could hear the horses coming across the valley. Their hoofbeats echoed
across the dried lake bed, and the early morning light was as brittle as if the
sun were layered with ice. Our horses stamped and blew silver vapor in the
cold. The desert looked like hammered copper, the dust spiraling into the
air. The posse kept coming and coming. One of the boys said, "Hell is just
a place you step into on an ordinary day." It was four weeks past the end
of everything.

Blood In My Eye

There's blood in my right eye
coming home from surgery.
It was my left eye
four years ago,
but not much changes.
The cataract is sucked out.
This is the way it happens.

A friend drives me home
in the red world.
My wife holds my hand.
I keep telling myself,
Everything's going to be
all right. I'm not
going blind. Believe it.

The First Cherry

I bring you the first cherry
from the tree in our backyard
in Yerington, Nevada.
The cherry is dark red, luscious,
about the size of a marble,
and the juice stains your lips,
your fingers. I go out
into the yard again,
plucking another cherry,
eating it in the kitchen.
Yuuum. Monday I gave you
a diamond to celebrate
30 years of marriage.
Could life get much better?

RONNIE M. LANE

Belly Song

The rhythm of the machines drowns out thought;
Erases my dreams with each clunk and whir.
My arms and hands move with the rhythm,
Part of the works, part of the mechanical whole
That constitutes the dreams and riches of someone else.
The burning in my shoulders replaces the burning
In my soul and the light in my eyes is
Fluorescent blue-green with artificial envy.
Conversation with strangers across the line
Has replaced friendship with shallow, bait-less
Fishing without a hook.
We brag about the sex we will be too tired to have;
The raft of our dreams will carry them out to sea,
To drown instead of finding paradise.
We speak about our children and grandchildren
Hoping their fate is different, knowing it will not be.
We go to church to hear about God's love
But the message is lost in the rumblings of our bellies.
Replacement parts arrived without notice;
The lump in my throat is reflux, not the awe

Of discovery or the glory of God.
Longing for fulfillment replaced
By the need for a break for lunch.
The bending of the future replaced
By the bending of my legs until they cannot bend once more.
Traded long ago the sunsets and walks along the beach;
There is only energy for a little tv and maybe a little more,
But no more than that. The sound of a shell against my ear
Is exactly like the sound of the electric motor by my side;
Except for the shell, and the sound of the sea.
More and more life becomes the snapshots of vacations
I used to take. More and more there is nothing worth remembering.
The fire in my belly is more liquor than inspiration.
The work is occupying like a cement truck,
Its spiral spilling toward the chute.
Not much thought is required, and after a while
Not much thought is given, if any.
We wonder where our job is tomorrow,
Sometimes literally. Sometimes there is no job.
We blame our government for letting them leave,
And we watch company after company go away.
We know the big picture and about how it all balances in the end.
But we don't want balance to come from our end,
And we don't want it to end at all.
Our fathers went to work at one job and retired
Grey-haired and well known by all.
We know we will work for 4 companies
That will go out of business while we work there;
Our grey hair does not come with dignity
Beyond the angle of our chins to the sky.

We are prisoners of the clock
Bound to it like a conjoined twin;
If it stops we do too, because time
Like the real world, is a dictatorship
And we don't get a vote.

The Cross Inside My Shirt

It is not tears, which will change the world,
the rumbling in our bellies to be fed,
the sound the wind makes winding
through the holes in our hearts.
If that worked we'd be lined up at the ocean

with our tin cups in our tired hands.
Neither will it survive because of us,
no amount of good-deed-doing,
tree hugging, tossing our aerosol deodorant in the trash.
If that worked, Babel would still reach up to heaven
and we'd be there having lunch with God and his kid.
Causes and becauses, stances and trances;
the doctor is a little slow; the patients have run amuck,
we want the sucker instead of the shot.
But a thought becomes a seed planted in the thoughts of others
and a cascade effect stabilizes into a torrent
sweeping away the old like dykes in a flood.
What will remain is the bedrock of earth,
which was never in danger, and unchanged throughout.

Fear Of Death

The edge of the lake is a shifting ribbon of mud;
The springtime waterline has turned into a beach;
Not the kind people lay on, but a sandy mash
Of life and death with lake grasses and tiny shells
That hold the sounds of places they've never been.

New plants, immigrants and opportunists seeking
A new place to sink roots and raise families,
Have crept from the underbrush to the frontline
To occupy the buffer zone between water and land.
If they grow tall enough, soon enough, they will live.

Many trails run down the hills, under the branches,
Bending down the tall grasses; all end in a drink.
Tracks of hoofs and paws and claws
In the mud at the edge of the clear cold water
Tell of deer and woodland creatures and a bear.

Out over the lake another flock of ducks circles,
Each group landing from south to north.
There are many flights of them now
Feeding and resting re-grouping
Migrating to winter feeding grounds.

The oaks have nearly shed their leaves now
November frosts and tans them soft brown
And they cover the trail with their scent.

Now the pines begin to assume command
Of the forest as others nod off to sleep.

The fall rains have begun, gently, cold.
The yellow maple leaves on the forest floor
Are matted, unable to sop up any more.
One morning a frost will seal the earth
And winter will finally begin.

World In Soft Orange

Idle winds take the time
to examine both sides of each leaf;
the tree for its part flutters
in a swaying circle dance.

Settling sun casts a smoldering shadow,
golden like a halo, writhing like a fire;
two people holding hands, walking by
appear to be angels against the dusky sky.

Smells of summer, quiet evening sounds,
a cat stretches and curls in a window.
Children playing in the streets,
safe in front of their houses.

Night sneaks up again.
Leave the couch, go to bed.
Darkness opens just enough eyes
to watch us while we sleep.

Weather Advisory Winter 08

One went high and one went low
And I saw them both from down below

I.
The storm winds came first, crawling,
sweeping lost snow like dirt, across the ground.
In clouds and mists and crawling vapors
the snow migrated across the road.
No notice taken that this was a boundary

or that those who had built it, must stay on it.
In obvious fiscal failure the assets of one snow bank
were transferred to the bank across the street.
The frozen wind dropped a lid of ice
on the boiling, over flowing river.
The ditches along the road
were stiff with relief and success.
The Great Lakes drink all winter;
the difference between a drought
and a draught is the ahh in the middle.

II.
The morning sun, yellow on the roof tops,
chases night into the blue shadows.

Strong   !   strobe
  light   strikes
       as   !   you
drive   past
  dark   !   trees

Six startled red cardinals
sunning at the roadside
seek shelter in low shrubs
beyond sight, by flight.

Sunshine washes in one side
then the other of the car
creating the sensation of movement
beyond the turning of wheels.
The tires sing a little harmony with the radio;
later, for the sad song, they sizzle through water.

DONALD LEV

I Blame This One On The Heat And Humidity, But
Apologize Anyway

I walked along this stream, fish kept biting my feet.
But it was cool and stony and I was
involved with nature.

These birds suddenly flew up into a branch of
a tree just above my head.
There was something strange about them.
They were red feathered wide eyed and had these
really bad teeth sticking out of their beaks which made them
look silly even for birds.
They eyed me in a funny way and seemed to be laughing.
I just stood in the water and was miffed.
This wasn't what I expected from all those nature films I
watched on the nature channel or reading National
Geographic.

I looked around for a canoe to hail, but it started raining,
and you know how hard it is to hail a canoe when it's raining.
Now I began to realize what a pickle I was in. I got out my
cell phone, thank god I had a cell phone, and called my office for help.
I did have an office, thank god, an office and a cell phone, otherwise
I would really find myself with a problem I could not solve.

Well, thank god I survived the wilds.

I don't know what else to say on this subject, except
that I should probably choose a different subject next time I write.

Reality

A total blanket of fog.
A screen totally blank.
Perhaps something is behind this.
Perhaps not.
I won't be the one to find out.

East of Eden

I don't live in the neighborhood.
Sorry.
I'm lost too.
I wandered down this rather boring main street,
then I turned up one street
and down another.
Which I shouldn't have done, with my
notorious lack of a sense of direction.

Now I am somewhere, I guess.
It looks like most other places.
Any town or any city.
A McDonalds a Burger King a
Rite Aid drug store.
The street's pretty wide and it's called Washington Street.
There is a traffic light, and several cars going each direction, so
I guess it is a large town or a city.
I begin to wonder what I thought I was doing here.
Then I just thought how my feet hurt.
It will be daylight soon.
I hope I can avoid the quicksand.

To A Friend

Sunshine, blue skies, suddenly
darken. People are like that too.
God I didn't think I'd be so moved
when the sunshine of your visage turned that blue
I mean prune blue tear stained blue
I know what pain is. That's all I can legitimately say to you.

National Holiday

The 4th of July has come and gone again.
I've yet to get hold of one of those American flag lapel pins
that all the politicians wear, and now Obama does too.
He rally wants to be in with the in crowd, in the worst way.
I don't really have a lapel to put a pin in anyway.
I used to have a blue suit jacket with a lapel into which
I had stuck a silver shoe with a hole in it given me
by the Volunteers for Stevenson for being such a
good volunteer. It burnt up with the rest of
my employer Cicero Codina's shoe store
in 1968, a year of many interesting conflagrations...

My computer has crashed. But tomorrow I get to
go to a barbecue. I feel such patriotism!

Sometimes I feel like a morally blind person
trying to feel my way out of a dark dripping cave.
But not today.

LYN LIFSHIN

The Terrible Dream

I've won a prize. There are several winners and
we are to give a reading when we get our award.
We have to read poems on a theme so I won't
read anything I have before, don't have
comfortable words that I know will work. I
know it will be odd reading new poems but
I can't say no. My dead mother and father are
alive and coming with me. We get there too
early. I want to explore the stage, get a feel. But
we are so early we decide after I read the poems
to my mother a few times, we will check in-
there's a hotel in the same square. Convenient
I shower, change my clothes a few times, not
sure what to wear. It's still too early. 2 hours
before the 7 o clock event I decide to lie down. We
have had something to eat. My mother and I share
the bed and my father is on the couch in the other
room as he usually was. I'm nervous, maybe some
aspirin with codeine. No reading seems easy but
with Mother and Ben here too. Somehow, I fall
asleep, escape maybe and when I wake up, the clock
says 7:30- Every one else is sleeping. I yank on my
boots, yell to them and am out the hotel door,
tearing to the stage where all the lights are already
turned off. The last person in the audience's is gone.
Only a few empty Styrofoam cups on the floor, not as
empty as I am

The Dead Are Too Loud

It could be passing
Arlington Cemetery
where the one I should
have flecked off me
like a moth, or those
dark ants that dropped
on the quilt from
varnished cherry,

85

clanks bone under his
last bed. Green this
spring instead of blue
sheets are often in
rain. The world from
the metro, splashed
water, something
slippery as light
flops up against, a
fish soon in a different
world, still, beginning
to rot. Later I dream
the dead into my
kitchen with only
the sound of my cat
on tile, these
words like
strangers in a
distance on a ship
that's sucked down
trying to tell you
what its like
before it happens

Black Sweater May

pulling the sun in close
that other May
the rose apple was
almost startling

I'd slept alone in
the west side of the
house, sloped
ceiling across the bed,
not wanting to hear
glass when a bottle
slammed thru it

The sun warmer
than hands, it slides
thru the last

mounds of snow as the
man who made me blush
just sitting near me

was suddenly there. I
hadn't seen him walking
toward where he'd
touch my shoulder,
tell me the name for
the tree I thought
was dogwood, pull

me toward his small
warm room that
night when it was
black and the grass
was black, wet, a
sweet smell I don't
remember smelling
since

Night Of Weird Dreams

I'm an artist, have done
a series of shadow boxes
that hang in a school or
a museum. Each has a
theme like in 5th grade
when each week some
one decorated a shelf.
I did a tapestry with
candles. Another time,
blue crepe paper, ballerina
dolls. Now the boxes are
a little like Joseph Cornell's
only the ones I do are
growing leaves and ferns,
moss. I bring the out
side inside to go with the
exhibit. I'm writing a
long piece. It's on my desk
when I get news that they
are carrying my art

out of the house with
rubber gloves. Someone
says there are insects
dripping from the frame,
a danger, a mess. Someone
tells me they are heading
for the dump. I jump
up, all the pages of my
article stupidly unnumbered
slither to the floor like
a hill of collapsed cards.
Then the words fall
off the pages

This December

A swan moved into the house, camouflaged among geese. She must have
been, or the mist from the pond blurred her. I say her because her antics
never seemed male. Never threatening, but coy. And never loitering on my
side of the bed. I suppose she was cold or starved. This year, the pond
froze early. When I think back, I remember a white feather on the deck but
that wasn't so strange. The tangerines were gnawed before they were ripe.
It could have been crows or

gulls I told myself after the space between my lover and I in bed got wider.
He thought this ghost bird was lovely as he had psychotic ballet dancer
lovers who became swans. The quilt's full of feathers he'd insist when a
pale wreathe of her circled the sheets. I thought it was more like something
wild staking territory. It wasn't that we really saw her though it is clear the
cat did. She was more of a presence and haunting as a dead love whose
handwriting lures and chills. I felt

her watch him. She knew his moods, each move and had more time to plot
seduction than I did. Being unattainable didn't hurt. He felt her breath
and his blood couldn't sleep. Drugs hardly helped but for once, he didn't
mind not sleeping. When he turned up music too loud for me, she moved
into his arms downstairs. I kept typing. I could feel her legs sprawled open
like a dancer with a miracle 180 degrees arabesque, hardly human, a wild
open grin. Crumbs

and bread disappeared. There were more feathers. It was like a mist and
the moon was hazy through her as if a storm was coming. Once when I
opened an old quilt from Odessa the room filled with its snow. Some days

seemed as opaque. The day the pond froze for good the house felt
somehow different. The cat stopped being spooked. A downstairs window
looked splintered but then I saw it was only frost etched in what looked like
a hieroglyph, something in a

language I don't know. I vacuumed up the last feathers. The stain of wings
still hangs in the air, gives the room a bluish light. Still, her leaving wasn't
like a break up where someone leaves the house, packs a painting, favorite
gloves but more the way something comes apart, as it did, so slowly it's
hard to tell when what isn't wasn't still whole

Images Of My Cousin

haunt the way
in certain light
or when wind comes
up behind
something dead
on the highway
it moves still,
seems alive.
In dreams my
cousin is
thin again,
giggling hasn't
called the police,
spit, "selfish
bitch." July is
lilacs still
in the cold hills.
August hasn't
exploded like
pieces of a
scattered bird

The Mad Girl Dances The Demons Out, Or
Tries To

if she could Rumba the blues
out, crackle of hips, a hiss,
a strut, a slow blood fire to
burn out what haunts her

Or maybe a tango would do it,
the love hate dance, the
flaming swivel, boot and heel
click stomping out cobalt

She wants to grind out
blackness, a foxtrot skid along
sanding terror, her dance shoe's
leather squashing the bad things

She's fierce to dance, a wild
fever, wants to fan and
hypnotize, the Braille of her
body, the SOS that seethes

this flesh Dear John E Mail
to the bluest blue blues

ELLARAINE LOCKIE

Voice Over

Not by chance that European chocolate
embedded with bits of coffee bean
was melting in my mouth
As your first spoken words
found their way from phone
to a tight fit in my ear canal

Fate pulling another part
of the puzzle that is you
Out of airwaves and into
the emptiness of need
The piece pairing perfectly
with the bittersweet fix
that scales the slope of my throat

Ground coffee beans
texturing burnished liquid silk
Like your gravelly timbre
vibrating in baritone smooth browns

Dialect slightly foreign
The effect like caffeine
from an 80% chocolate bar

Time Bomb At O'Hare Airport

I'm in America now
So get the hell out of my way
Window-rattles the woman
disembarking our British Airliner
when teenagers block the exit

Her escape from the holiday prison
of polite protocol
Where people pacify savagery
with purrs of *Please and Pardon me love*
Diffusing devises lost on the woman

Whose pressure cooker must be chock-full
from childhood forward
With foul-mouthed fill-ins for life's letdowns
that explode in the face of any obstacle
Like the boys who crowd the corridor

Through which the woman shoves
bags bulging with Paddington Bears
Peter Rabbits and Cadbury's chocolates
for grandchildren watching at the gate
Waiting to engender the next generation
of social graces

Godot Goes to Montana

My farmer father waited to see
if crops would hail out or dry up
If coyotes would tunnel the chicken coops
If the price of grain could keep
me out of used clothes
If the bank would waive foreclosure
for another year

After hay baling and breech delivering
from sunrise to body's fall
He slept in front of the evening news
Too worn out to watch the world squirm
Too weary to hear warnings from ghost brothers
who were slain by beef, bacon and stress
Too spent to move into the next day

when he couldn't afford to forget
how Brew Wilcox lost his left arm to an auger
How the mayor's son suffocated in a silo
Too responsible to remember the bleak option
my grandfather chose for the rope
hanging over the barn rafters

Never too lonely because every farmer
had a neighbor to bullshit with
To share an early a.m. pot of Folger's
To eat fresh sourdough doughnuts
To chew the fat of their existence

First appeared in *SLAB*.

Solar Power on the Prairie

Here with the certainty that sun
climbs the Bear's Paw Mountains every morning
I return to the warmth each summer
Walk the prairie roads
when the sun's hands touch mountain's top

When they open perfume
on purple clover blossoms
Polish pheasant feathers to a spit shine
And snap the stereo switch
that sets roosters and meadowlarks to music

A Chinook from the west
turns wheat into soft wind chimes
And cottonwood leaves
bend their ears into the whispers
While Cree ten miles east
talk to their God at this time every a.m.

The farmers rise and pray for rain clouds
to cry over dust depressed crops
But I welcome the hands of dawn
How they wander over my unbuttoned body
Strip the gray from daybreak
Stain my skin a kindle wood brown
Inject the fuel to burn for another year

First appeared in *The Aurorean*.

Scene of the Crime

I see them from my driver's license
on top of the garbage-can overflow
Their five, two and one-year-old paper faces
next to me in the trash
Taking in the rust stains around the sink
and the yellow smell from the urinal
Their innocence autonomous in this back alley
sex shop bordered bathroom

Footpaths of toilet paper
map the underlying filth
My leather wallet lays forsaken on the floor
A splayed animal flattened
by the hit and run of a thief
Who lingered long enough to strip the flesh
and discard anything not consumable

I watched my cash pay its way into his pocket
The contribution of credit cards
and Christmas gift certificates
All through the eyes of a DMV saint
But as he finger-stuttered smudges
over the photos of my grandchildren
These eyes narrowed to arrows
that pierced the paper with permission
on a license to kill

Where There's Smoke. . .

There's a Starbucks man
Lips encircling a cigarette

in James Dean demeanor
Suckle love chiseling his cheekbones

And I inhale simultaneously
Sharp and shallow
Unlike him and his lazy draw
two tables away
Unaware of my ill-mannered stare
Of his smoke signals that send
seductive language to like kind

Silent alarms sounding
more than secondhand smoke warnings
Flashbacks of Salem cigarettes
and other stale hungers burn fresh
And the saint of safety
is supplanted by devil-may-care

I wonder whether his hands
are as hazardous
as the come-hither nicotine
Whether the heat rising from my belly
is vicarious or lascivious

Either way I want to cut and run
Coffee half consumed
Leave the cravings commingled
with caffeine in the cup
Instead I stay spellbound
Die-hard held by old conflicts
Clichéd as a moth to flame

Caffeine combining with compulsion
And with questions like
Will I outlast his next light-up
Listen to life in long-term whispers
Or will I banish hazards to hell
And burn in the fire of gratification
Its short fuse a live-out-loud
shout of fortitude

Run-On Sentence

Maybe it's easier to accept if you aren't

ambivalent, if you hadn't loved him
more than life itself, if he hadn't hurt you in a
forever way then went and died without
saying he was sorry or even good-bye,
leaving only unfinished feelings to fight
your fears of vulnerability, those toxic chemicals
tainting capacity to care, adulterating every
romantic relationship you'll ever have until
you reconcile the eternal reality that a ghost
can't repent and you have to become your
judge who vindicates you with a not-
guilty verdict by reason of a child's innocence.

GERALD LOCKLIN

What I Learned From Athletic Competition

That you can always do more
Than you (or others) think you can,

And that the human body can produce
Its own chemistry of
Excitement and Tranquility.

And, as a fan, that sports talk can,
Like Literary and Cinematic Criticism,
Philosophy, Theology, or
Sociopolitcal Disputation,

Go beyond Bullshit, Moralizing, and Insult,
To the pleasures of informed, intelligent,
Analytical, creative, experientially grounded, and
Idiomatically diverse yet sophisticated discourse.

In other words: Intellectual Fun.

André Kertész: Circles and Curves

The most obvious of the latter are,
Or course, in his signature photograph of
The *Satiric Dancer*, curled in gleeful

Quasi-bondage on a well-worn sofa in the
Corner of the studio, and flanked,
On trapezoidal walls, by the sculpture of
A twisting male torso - perhaps an ancient
Athlete - and a painting of a bosomy and
Full-hipped naked female. Even the page of
newsprint tacked above her leans with flight
And gravity out of its rectangle.

Sexual attraction is a centripetal force.

You find it also, though, in *Chez Mondrian*,
Where the brimmed hat on the wall,
The vase of yawning flowers, and
The spiral staircase (you are always in a different
Spot yet in a previously traveled longitude)
Controvert the man-made grids for which the resident
Genius grew famous.

Even the cantileverage of the *Eiffel Tower* depends
Upon a Romanesque musculature, whereas the
Rectilinear bridge and building of the *Pont Des Arts*
Is viewed through the transparent circularity of a
Clock whose hour-hand is a gear form which
Extends a star.

The paths of the snowed-in *Washington Square*
Slalom in solitude past the crescent guard-rails.

Every item (every atom) in Kertesz conspires on
Behalf of the organic versus the unyielding:
McDougal Alley disappears beneath the
Tenements: no faces gaze from even the
Best-lit of windows. The snow, now general even
Over Irish-America, will soon be thawed to
Cinders by the 1960s. A *Fork* and its concave shadow
Make praying/preying mantids upon the lip, the lisp,
The shadow of a freshly polished, welcoming,
And pudentatious bowl. The solitary commuters
Between the *Poughkeepsie* tracks have descended
Iron stairs onto a regimented, platformed silence,
Looking past each other towards the insignificance
Of passing, wasted life-time. And on a rainy day in
Tokyo, ties and umbrellas form a snaking queue along
The linearity of Time's relentless, unforgiving arrow.

The *Seine* and *Quais* are parallel commercial
Freeways (bless the resilient Parisians for somehow
Romanticizing the Modern, a feat like rendering
Rotted meat to delicacies, the magic of the
Butcher and the Saucier).

Even the human,
When stretched to sinew
Like the *Underwater Swimmer*,
Has the deathly pallor of the drowned
Upon it.

Only the blown sails of *The Homing Ship*
And the tree which flowers towards infinity of sky
And depths of the reflecting April rainpool
Offer hope of seasonal renewal, that time does
Bend back on itself eternally, as flesh draws
Flesh into its own inexplicable resurrection.

Vincent Van Gogh: Postman Joseph Roulin,1888

Can we ever look too often
At a painting by Van Gogh?

Perhaps, but not this one.

I read Van Gogh's description of
"A man who is neither embittered.
Nor sad, nor perfect, nor happy,
Nor always irreproachably right...
But such a good soul and so wise
And so full of feeling and so truthful,"

And I hearken back to when,
A teenager, I read *Dear Theo,*
Vincent's letters to his brother,
And I see the words embodied in
The postman's face, beard, hands,
Blue uniform and cap, blue eyes, blue sky,
All Blues, No Blues, Eternal Verity of Blue,

And suddenly it strikes me that,
My God!—Van Gogh was no less

Poet than he was a painter—
He even anticipated the parataxic style
That Juan Gris and Picasso
Passed to Gertrude Stein,
From whom Ernest Hemingway
Adapted and perfected it.

I bet if you'd handed him
A saxophone, he would have
Metamorphosed into Coltrane,
Vanished into the exultative choruses
Of *A Love Supreme.*

B.Z. NIDITCH

A Poet in Exile
for John Berryman

Off the Cape,
you are a dead weight
while a stormy night
wrestles sharp-toothed demons,
you cannot sleep alone
whispering into a bleeding pillow,
"Restore me, your Johnnie,
from my tangled past,
exchange me for objects d' art
and impressions at auction,
puncture me with pleasure,
wound me again
with 'Dear John' letters
in missives I'll throw
into abandoned stalls
marked with ink stains
and telephone numbers."

In Greenwich Village

Feeling the apartment doors
bathtub of running water
and Coltrane

close on you, Josephina,
from a leather mood
the old cinnamon cat sings
down the broken third step
you ruffle up
the Russian priest
down on his luck
holding a doggy bag
full of Chinese fortune cookies.

The ex-diva now turned pro
screams under city lights
in the knotted sleet
you search for change
for a curbside omelette
or fallafel,
a red sports car crashes
flowers from first communion
and the newly risen Doctor Mojo
the never tongue-tied ladykiller
passes Josephina
once his theosophy matchmaker
who has had no success stories
in twenty years
now ready to pawn
her ex-husband's violin case
full of hair and rosin
where memory once had good eyes
playing for tomorrow.

Sandscript: Martha's Vineyard

The wind trembles like ochre dreams
a cat circles your footsteps
reproaching us
for getting lost
near the lighthouse
among an arabesque of islands
off the Vineyard's sea
a snapshot gone
in twenty-one seconds
forgetting the dialogue
more affectionate

than a July morning
choosing the friendship
of Earth's fruitful sand
you hide an apple
in a pirate's hat
you wore till night
playing solitaire
under an immeasurable moon
listening to a tape of Coltrane
in a faithful daze
a blue heron appears
undreaming the twilight
with an unreasonable laugh
taking off again
on an ill advised town
with no destiny behind
the parched parkway trees
feeling uninvited by nature
reproached by sailboats
out beyond the water depths
unresponded to making beds
out of the tall grasses.

Somewhere Ulysses

On the boundless shore
your voice still leaves
your shadows gone
drifting forgettably
in skiffs
like blackbirds
you are snatched up
on the pitched deck
from high loud speakers
lifeguard's summon
by the sunlight's passing hours
on ionian radio waves
blaring out like crows
on empty white sand
all the swallowed up excitement
in beaches of our exile
on crystalline waters
you drift and sweep

on glittering tall ships
over the bronze home harbor

The Quiet Ones

You say you can spot them
anywhere,
by their eyes, expression, skin,
colorful dress
but it is your monologue
which approaches
in an imperfect time
or an unimaginable hour
from a meagre age
that you first heard
there is no room
or meal
for them;
write it down,
say it never happens
that you never knew
or met them face to face
it must be someone else
some other place
it occurs, never here.

In The Cellar

Growing down to size
you were not allowed
sunlight, even to dust
off the grand piano,
*It might spoil
the furniture*, Mother Cold
said when you muzzled
a carnation
in a buttonhole
behind the cellar's
threadbare curtain.

You hid smoking pipes,
red boas,

and a pirate's earring
in perfumed boxes
above execution living rooms
of untouchable sofas
full from blanket kitsch,
licking stamps and copper coins,
to address and uncover,
to send you away.

March Blues

Bird Parker plays
from an empty street,
dusky flakes emerge
through Venetian blinds,
you eye backyard crows
on elm, pine, and poplar,
bliss stares from the sky
even at winter's height,
ivory showers drift about
ridiculous March clouds.

Putting a favorite denim
on the capsized iron chair
you resist staring
at the doorway's open umbrella,
Salt and Pepper catwalk
round the wood stove,
a voice mumbling on the line
calls up names and dates
that escape your memory
like the lucent snow outside,
your life restarts
its second nature.

SIMON PERCHIK

*

Another trench :my fist opened
--the dirt that struck your lid
already rebuilds the world

--with that first damp thud
you begin to breathe the way a flower
blossoms and the sky growing back

--you think something fell from a wall
--that old photograph where everyone
is smiling and you try again

but your lips --what you hear
is the beginning, for the first time
a far off breeze returns

where your breath still clings
to moonlight and your lips
covered over with hillside

by the handful, bringing you
more black, flesh that absorbs
what the light lays down to start again

as shadow --I bring you
the nest some tree might dig
--by the handful your bones

warmed by this sound taking hold
its leaves, its skies and the dirt
even in winter, even between my fingers.

*
Pulling the mirror closer
till an old love note
almost ignites again

--even two suns are not enough
changing colors
just for the fragrance

her breasts give off.
She cups her mirror
the way a sundial winds down

and the light slows for evening
--you will recognize these beauties
the golden shoulders now invisible

brushed among the leaves and cinders
filling her arms with arms, eyes
with eyes and your fingers on fire.

*

The dead branch writing on this wall
never learns --a name
could change things, pleaded with
the way a steady rain
softly from among the others
reaches down to promise in writing

--all summer and the name
hardly begun, the bare tree
grieving for the one name
whose shadow is the sky all night

taking so long --the leaves
couldn't hold on any more
and what's left little by little
the wall becomes your name
broken in pieces.

*

At night and this beach bathed
as if it had two mothers, half sand
half stench and loving you

till your still soft heart
and the sun survives
by hiding, seeps from the surface

and the devouring light - - in the dark
you will learn to splash
sooner than the others

get the jump, each shoulder
rinsed, taught to cool
and this great ocean from inside.

*

Now that the sky is homeless
you make your own season
and each morning for just a minute

the snow is not mentioned
- - even in summer you set aside
one window for tracks, covered over

and the wind hiding in bells
- - you use this makeshift silence
the way a rifle is still aimed

with a deep breath and hold
- - it's not for long, your season
sets up and from its rivers

a blackness flowing, gathering
first as a rain that is not the sky
- - it's new for you, a sister-season

open and bleeding :a minute
rescued from the others
and at each funeral it shows up

ready to party, still young
though you cry out loud for a mouth
for the air that will not come.

CHARLES P. RIES

Hearing Perfectly

"You're missing all the high pitched, soft consonant
sounds," the audiologist told me.
 "You mean women's voices?"
 "Well, yes I guess you could say that."

Isn't it odd, how men suffer this deafness?

We stare intently with sympathetic smiles watching
their lips shower us in sentences half heard.

I've noticed that missing so much of what she tells me
has deepened my affection for her.

Is this what they mean by making more out of less?

El Latino Blanco
(The White Latin)

I woke throughout the night as the fleas kept biting my toes.
Just my toes - the rest of me didn't seem to interest him.

"El Latino Blanco" the bartender called me as I ordered double
shots of tequila throughout the night, one for me and one for my
friend, the large white rabbit I call El Conjito Blanco Grande
who sat invisibly next to me, as he has next to other drunks
who use him as an excuse to order doubles.

My dreams that night were ones of desolation and consolation.
I remember because the fleas kept me on the edge of real time.
Maybe they weren't fleas at all, but insect sized psychic miners,
biting me to lucidity and injecting me with some sort of
drunken-poet-dream-sex-venom.

As the morning came, the fleas went to sleep and I drifted away
on a deep cool river, waking to a pure blue sky, a massive
Mexican hangover, and the smell of black coffee served by a
mescal worm named Little Rico.

Just Some Days

15th / Ides of March

> Sick with the flu; and a good day to celebrate the
> treachery of politicians. Elaine told me, "You needed
> to get sick." (*What does she mean by that?*).

> Had soup with dry toast; went to bed early.

16th / My Birthday

Slept late, and woke feeling better. Skipped the gym.
Got a hair cut (*Had to take shit from Bob the Barber;
harassment comes free with the service.*)

Elaine sent me a provocative birthday card (*she knows
how stuff like that gets me going.*) She said, "You've got lots of
testosterone for a guy your age, who cares if you're losing your
hearing. You're usually more worried about sex than listening
anyway."

Bought a pizza, watched March Madness, had a beer.
Never though turning 55 would be this nice.

17th / Saint Patrick's Day

Drove past a bunch of drunks at 8:00 a.m. on Water
Street. "It's an American Drinking Holiday," I tell my
daughter. We drive around talking about bands and
listen to music. She's 17, wise, and tells me, "You
still look a lot younger than 55, who cares if you're
shrinking and your ears appear to be growing."

I'd be Patrick if my mom had waited fifteen minutes to give
birth, but I guess some of us just aren't born lucky.

My life became poetry when I started writing it in stanzas.

Seeing Nothing

Jeannie tall, thin
husky voice, sees visions.
Jeannie with the light brown hair,
lives in a bottle soft and quiet.

*People are like snow flakes, aren't they?
Each a different shape.
All of them falling to the ground in exactly their way.*

John large and round,
loud slow river moving.

A log in the forest - fallen
decomposing - compost for renewal in spring.

People are like leaves, aren't they?
Each a different color.
Each uniquely blown by an invisible breeze.

Alice large breasted, thin hipped
making the guys trip as she walks by;
doing well in a cloak of beauty she did not ask for,
doing well to remember what's important in life.

People are like finger prints, aren't they?
Each leaving a different impression
on life's glass top.

Bill's mind blazes.
Ideas eat his sleep
compelling him to create,
like a dreamer gone mad.

People are invisible, aren't they?
What we see tells us nothing.

In This Movement Of Air

We stand in twilight
knowing meaning will
come as it always does.

Some things are beyond our
control:

> The migration of birds
> The end of love
> The Harvest moon
> The inevitability of war

Some things just happen.

This ebb and our flow are as
fixed and predictable as the
certainties of gravity.

Raising our eyes toward the night
sky we embrace beneath a rain
of falling leaves, and celebrate
the autumn of our time here.

This Land Within

Breathing silently
       deeply
          pausing
The quiet embraces

Sunlight is hidden today

Autumn fields
Freshly turned
Corn once rooted here
Now a playground for crows

A moment
       to see
         stillness

In a gray cascading mist
Thoughts are placed into soil
Hibernation in dream time

Walking on
       empty
        clear
         light
Wind at my back
Helping me home

LYNNE SAVITT

It's Different

now it's approaching seven
& the lines at local restaurants

are mounting you think i'll crumble
with desire to sit in a cushy booth
with warm crusty bread in a basket
running my finger down endless
selections of veal, chicken, eggplant

longing for a a slice of cheesy pizza
served on the red formica counter
icy diet coke with lemon or a margarita
guacamole salsa chips or by the water
my favorite table bloody mary shrimp
cocktail garlicky scallops salad with
goat cheese & walnuts raspberry vinaigrette

think white tablecloth a wood smoked thick
slab of steak buttery corn thai dressing
on fried calamari i love dinner out any
where drive through a few square steamed
hamburgers white castle of my dreams
our favorite pastime dining together you
think i'll crumble for the dinner hour

it's different this time i won't give in for
sustenance that never fills me i'll
gorge on dry saltless pretzels finally
acknowledging no dinner supreme or
endless with you can ever fill me
what an empty booth we fill together
does anyone know we're there?

Love Don't Pay The Bills

stifling august afternoon shopping
on royale street hot as remoulade
we dipped cold shrimp in lazy lust
i asked you to take me there
where you ask camilla's grille by
streetcar or pirate's cove for blues
& bloody marys no i answer take me
there you light a joint & pass it to me
strolling past harrah's crowds of elderly
& poor glued to slot machines looking
like antique cast iron toys with moving

parts of me know i belong back home
but please take me there i plead again
& somehow after you spill a sugary pink
hurricane down my sheer white blouse
you kiss my neck & pull cool blonde
strands of hair twirled around your silver
ringed fingers yr guitar at house of blues
salty fries left on a plate of take me
there in an alley with music shaking
us humid vibrating & pressed hard against
wall of receipts blow away with the wind
my purse falls mastercard floats in oil
slicked puddle let me fall here i belong
in this city anyone can lose themselves
in splendor & gumbo i cannot go home
take me there i'll wait tables & you can
play 3 a.m. gigs to pay the rent or let
go of my arm & give me back to new
york where money & marriage call

November Home At Last

time i spoke to you my father
was in rehab now another
operation on hip became dis
placed his skeletal fiingers
reach up like ET's phone
home at last you are where
i can picture you can't believe
he hasn't eaten in weeks &
now there's talk of death how
do people do this mother not
willing to help me, baby, can i
run away will you let me come
back to you new orleans still
wobbly like eighty five year old
broken hip struggling to walk
again i ask you let me come
static on phone line i hear
clinking glasses laughter loud
music it's 3 a.m. & you don't
hit the sheets until 5 songs
i don't recognize beat i do

say sleep sweet & let receiver
fall to carpeted floor me be
there this time when i need
you not to enter me like a train
but shelter me like a good beige
cashmere fur trimmed coat

Digging Dinosaur Dignity In Ardortown

the chimp wearing candy apple red lipstick
& an armani tuxedo warms rolls of toilet paper
in the micorwave valentines day is almost here
i love you daddy down in the snow covered
grave goings on in the house you worked so
hard to keep mother an eighty one year old
child i care for how dare you leave us speech
less parkinsons destroyed your brain & no sour
gummy bears or thick coffee shakes could bring
you back to all of us visited cried tried to help i
scream help it's fallen apart like a first marriage
bitter chocolate lessons you would be proud
your funeral was just what you wanted military
honor guard guns banging frigid snowy air white
valentines kissed the dirt & we stood frozen tears
worn like crystal accents tiny family together
accolades for you keep coming how pleased you'd
be a scholarship in your name me one to care for
mother dirty trick i can hear you cackling now
where can we find dignity of living long enough
for diapers & dribbling yr tiny mouth forming words
that couldn't be translated pain becomes ecstasy
as long as we suffer we're alive to excavate fossils
of world war two & ardor town we wished we knew
you when you lived there dreaming of mother in
her blue bathing suit & kisses you'd never imagine
would dry up faster than a wet beach towel in
arizona sun fades behind new york winter clouds
we miss you daddy gone one month we miss
feeling safety gone i am the older child & own
two remaining cemetery plots where no one will
reside in water is where i want my ashes how
did it come to this january weeping daddy dead

Love Song If I Could Sing

for you the music plays for
me ordinary woman storing
warm wool socks & chocolate
pops for grandchildren growing
faster than peach summer light
fades dull cold mornings the
warmth i seek is you for who
the music plays for me ordinary
woman turning sixty blonde
hair some parts silver love me
tomorrow when wet is a memory
& juice that kept us vibrant no
longer keeps us churning man
for you the music plays for me
ordinary woman becomes song

The 5,298TH Poet's Poem For A 60th Birthday

summer of my 60th birthday
fireflies return with a vengeance
to light the dark warm skies
universe of miniature fireworks
not since i was ten & we caught
them in jelly jars have nights
twinkled with this buttery glow

my children settled with spouses
houses near the ocean what
more could a mother want
surf sounds of contentment

my granddaughter almost
as tall as i love to see her
bloom little 12 yr old peonies
dance on her soccer playing
torso strong bloodline petals

for all those years i thought
poetry was life
my life was poetry
& now there is only life

what a cold blue change
in my red hot world

wake up & smell melting
decades of lovers lost
to cancer & cross county
moves younger pussy
memory burns me to
them & them to me

happy, happy birthday
baby the song goes &
so do I

Labor Day Weekend 2007

we choose a seaside
restaurant second floor
glass & dark wood panels
sitting inside birds' eye view
below of bustling crowd outside

sunburned waitress in tank top
with waist length blond hair
carries beers to scruffy shirt
less group with backwards
blue baseball caps sucking

fresh clams & oysters on ice
loud music & laughter paint
the last weekend of summer sky

turns dark wind picks up rain
starts to hit the glass panels

tray above her head nipples
poke through wet white shirt
others scurry for cover
i sip a french martini

was it yesterday we would have
been out in the rain smell of sun
tan lotion & spilled beer as we

pressed against the wooden
shack for joyful cover?

you say how lucky we are
safe & dry clams oregenata
waiter in pressed black pants
brings warm bread & ice water

do you want to walk in the rain
i ask you order coffee & trimisu
i pat my lips with the linen napkin
blow a kiss to busboy & head
for hurricane night calling
me don't offer an umbrella
what i need wet love even
if only in memory saves

us from what we've become
& kisses our chapped lips
with protected dreams of
what we once were

Poem For My Son On The Birth Of His First Child, Kylie Lane Newton, 4/13/2008

a month before your 38th birthday
she comes early in april diamond
birth stone sparkles yr life alive
the way you did mine emerald may
of 1970 i couldn't ask more for you

than this grace of green velvet love
reupholstering your nights like a greedy
scarlett o'hara dressed in drapes
helpless we are to save our precious

children will lead you save you make
you ride the horse of an amethyst color
what you won't do for her this little pearl
who changed the hue of downtown dawns

quartzite pink skies & glass castles of wall
street king of kylie's dreams & mine

i get to watch this tale as you & your sister
& my grandchildren make this story your

own pierced belly buttons, tattooed lower
backs golden color, silver textures of dented
motorcycle fenders & peridot side trips
turquoise heartbreaks & citrine joys

finally i am ready for the treasured
endings of your semi precious
choices granny's quiet crown
of wisdom i gladly adorn

HARRY SMITH

Rites of Fall

I play each season's major symphony.
Its odors & tastes, colors, sights & sounds.
Now autumn & I meld a tapestry
Of life's slow burning, and the earth abounds
With fecund decay. I shall oxidize
Like blazing leaves. I shall be as *eiswein*
Sweet-tempered by the frost while the vine dies,
Or apples over-ripe: a rich design
Of rot & renewal, preparation
For the spring surge. I shall become compost.
Composition & decomposition
Are one, which is why I love the fall the most.

I fall laughing into soft sphagnum moss
Of fog forest: there is no waste, no loss.

Wild Geese

"Geese!"
            "Where?"
                        "In the sky,."
Silhouettes against a luminous snowcloud.
"Yes. Beautiful."
Why do we wonder at the common sight?

Our wistful spirits follow their arrow –
Is it our hearts' migrations too that we know?
                                    Their calls too far to hear
resound in mind.
Somehow we join the rhythm of their wings
                          aimed east
back to the age-old breeding grounds.

Pigeon

I meet, I pause, I pass such queer old books, whose names I know-
The Soul Of The White Ant. Do they have souls? Do we? Who knows?
Perhaps I need *The Public Life Of The Street Pigeon* now,
But what would it tell us of the pigeon who crossed our path,
Crisscrossing, back & forth, in front of us on the sidewalk
Outside our building. When we stopped, it walked up to my wife,
As if asking for help, a small spot of blood on its breast.
She ran upstairs, returned with a cardboard box and a towel.
She dropped the towel gently over him, put him in the box.
We could try to nurse him back to health and keep him safe. No.
He wouldn't last the night. So we took him in a taxi
To Animal Medical Center. "We've a hurt pigeon.
He's bleeding from the breast. Maybe he was hit by a car."
"Is he your pigeon?" asked a young man at the admissions desk.
"We found him in the street."
"We need the name of the owner."
"I'll pay," I said, imagining a thousand-dollar dove.
A young vet, writing a report, asked: "Whose pigeon is this?"
"It's everybody's pigeon. He's mine, if you need a name."
"We'll treat him if you leave him. But you can't call about him.
We'd turn him over to the wildlife conservation folks
To care for him until he's ready to be released, with luck."
The street pigeon book might tell us how many get killed by cars
Or fly into skyscrapers or get poisoned in the park.
Although we had no right to call, my wife did make the call.
No one knew anything about everybody's pigeon.
I picture him nevertheless in a pleasanter park,
The closest in his flock to an old lady feeding birds.

Whole Earth

To see the Earth from Space! My boyhood dream,
that thrilling trek come true, or partly true:
at least I share the splendid photographs.
I tried, applied to see it for myself.
– "A teacher or writer," NASA replied,
but sent the teacher to glorious death.
A planetarium show conveyed me
to the moon when I was eight. I leapt
deliriously in light gravity,
and when we bounced radar waves off the moon,
that touch convinced me we'd land there,
and soon enough we did. I was still young
enough, just part of that collective *we*,
and yet I felt like a participant.
More beautiful than imagination,
the pictures from the odysseys stir awe
primordial. I marvel most at Earth,
to look backward to see her whole,
this green world of oceans & living things,
the queen of planets – sovereign indeed!
Space flight returns us to our origins:
the Earth becomes our Goddess once again,
demanding we obey the laws of life.
Her powers override our poor tenancy.

The Garden of Questions

Autumn's vibrant hues:
or is it we who vibrate
in vivid rhythm

Am I Sisyphus?
Rake relentless leaves of fall
over & over

You know the lilac bloom & its perfume,
but have you seen the leaf's royal purple veins
or the lilac blush of its inner wood

Shall you find beauty
in the bill clicks of an owl
or the caws of a crow mob

Has the Earth ever
given us two dawns or twilights
that came the same

And time & again
will you marvel sadly
at Time's chariot

Can you find the poem
in the tamarack needles
turned golden in death

?
Does the question mark
hover in the frontal lobe
like Damocles sword

blue midnight   full moon
the tidal basins brimming:
do you hear the tune

When the winter sun
stays south, why does the moon shift
its course further north

Why all the twitter? —
snow buntings swirling like snow
onto sunflower seed heads.

How come the starry bear was limned
by Greeks & Amerindians —
the myth older than the races

For whom does the cock crow
Does he know

Tell me the meaning
of sharp sun striking straight through
ice crystal forest.

Life is the question —
yea, the question of questions.
Death is the answer.

Why do you find peace
when you lose yourself looking
across salt marshes

What is your weather
Do you feel like snow or rain
or bright ice that burns

If there be mind's eye,
shall I tell of my mind's tongue
tasting the rosebud

How many guises
has the One True God
of the Only Holy Faith

Can haiku hold
brick smokestacks and Romanesque towers
of Lowell's old mills

Is it a bad thing
to see everything as if
for the last time

Can you find the song
in the muck & mulch of spring
before snowdrops sing

So what if the moon,
Saturn & Regalus go
together tonight

Coming home in spring,
she asks which April evening
the tree frogs first trilled

JARED SMITH

A Mountain in a Suitcase

A computer makes you think
that you do not grow.
A computer takes your words,
burnishing each in time
each
single
one
in the context of a splinter.
Ragged
pulled away from its roots
festering under the skin...

an angry thought
interlaced with desire to grow
stands out forever
with no context.
Twenty years from now
who will remember
the context of words are
grunts
you make trying to build a life...

the shavings that you leave behind
are not you, but things that do not grow.
They are leave-behinds that leave you better
in the context they leave behind
outside the computer,
but inside the computer they are twisted seeds
stored without water waiting to grow
without the context...

They are your calls in the night to your lover
and your subnotes to yourself to help you grow
striking an electrostatic charge that freezes them.
And they are carried in the hearts of your children.
and they are carried in the heart of your pink slip
in the digital photo of your leaving work
they are no more than pixels
in a box that remembers every cry of anguish
out

of
context

a mountain that fills the night
is packed into a suitcase
going from streetlamp to streetlamp
in the hardened hands of a muttering old man.

Fine Bone China

You were walking between the campus buildings
bright dreams and warm woolly jackets between the buildings
long hair brown in the sunlight blowing in the wind
with books between the building at Kent State
when sharp reports that would fill your years forever thudded into flesh
driving out the color of your eyes and the color of the children
you taught in your class on *American Literature: Philosophy of
                                    Romanticism*
gunned down by the National Guard because they were carrying books
between classes on the campus of Kent State
instead of boxes of bullets in Vietnam.

You served me years later
bowls of home-made soup in your garden apartment in the Village;
and the soup was brewed from bones nestled in China,
from heavy American oxen from the Midwest
who lay down with a cleaver between their eyes
and filled the bowls you placed before us.

We couldn't fit our spoons down into the broth
between the bone and fine bone china.
They carried you away on Thorazine.

Symphony

A woman walks into a room with wooden planks for a floor.
        There are
                                three points
                    between her and
            her lover.
There are   three points
                    between her birth and

her death.
There is a mirror
          on the wall
                              that sees one way
    until she turns.

          There are three points between her
          and a name that puts men to death in uniform.
She does not know this.   There is only one point
between her   and the man who will hold her hand at death.
A rose bud fills a table. The world is small. The floor polished.
                    Dust floats across the mirror.

          She dances to a music no one else can see

Why Put Up With This Anymore?

Whether it is spoken words or written ones,
men cannot bring a people together to extract wealth from what is natural
men cannot pull iron or gold from the darkness that is earth,
men cannot shape steel to climb into the sky on cocktail wings,
men cannot herd men and girls into concrete towers
where nothing grows except their love for each other
men cannot grow corn or wheat or marijuana or cocaine,
men cannot turn water or fossil fuel to the fiery entertainment of electricity,
men cannot carry their ill-gotten produce from one town into another,
men cannot plant seeds with any expectation of what they will become,
men cannot drive down a highway with no car and no hard surface,
men cannot remember where they are going or that they are alone or not,
men cannot lead invincible armies with evolving weapons,
men cannot even feed themselves or their wives or children
without fluttering your lungs and your lips together
and without your fingers trembling on the edge of something great
and without growing up among others who likewise shape their lips around air,
telling stories that decide who will be the most inclusive mover of words,
whether journalists, engineers, generals, singers, politicians, or presidents,
there are ultimately no others who can come before you
whether it is by spoken words or written ones, Poet,
I cannot understand why you hang your head down
and skulk in alleys eating poverty with your words.

Ramses Visits The Cradle of Democracy

Struggling to comprehend the Museum of Anthropology and Archeology
from a gray grained room down the street from The Wharton School
in Philadelphia,
Ramses' *bas,* despite the university and museums, does not
speak economics.
He perceives a different kind of degrees, a muted room of Egyptian obelisks
and sphinxes;
He is himself the sphinx with five engravings of the pharaoh's name along
sand blasted sides.
His tail is strung around his haunches, along his back nearing his
sphincter muscles.
The *bas* thinks upon Benjamin Franklin and James Madison who crafted
Democracy nearby.
In the thinking, he goes weird. His head and shoulders that remained
above the sand
through centuries of lifeless erosion are worn beyond the strength of
his testicles;
his face no longer Ramses, but a grey elephant. His beard is the trunk,
his headpiece the ears.

His eyes are the blank of egg-beaters, the formaldehyde of Dickey's
Sheep Child
personified in sandstone. He is the centerpiece, looking out through the
musculature of a
cat until the shadows fall; for then his life comes out and inhabits the
living, after dark.
It draws energy from the city streets, the troubadours, the call girls,
penny ante stuff
that is all that he can see, for his *spiritus mundi* travels and partakes only
at night:
Not sheepish in the least, it partakes of what he sees and believes is the
best, poor tired king.

America, you are left behind upon mummified wings.
A half block away, the draft cover page of Darwin's *Origin of Species*
is on Display.
Linnaeus charts the sedimentary layers of history. The shop shuts
down at four.

Father,

your grandson is struck sterile
among choices you have left behind.
The compass that carried you through Eagle Scouts is gone;
the badges worn across your chest, dust like the degree from Harvard.
I am a cold point beneath the winter sky,
a dust mote upon a string played *obligate* between galaxies,
and soon enough there will be no mountain meadows
for your descendants to walk among.

Darkness burns away on the wings of a moth
flaring itself into a place you have come to know.
The maples I climbed on have gone,
with no more power in their roots to shade your window.
The driveway I carried your suitcase along that last day
has been blacktopped three times that I know
and the weeping cherry you never knew was planted
by my son whom you never knew
and dwarfs a house on the other side of town.

You knew the lady slippers and May apples,
showed me where tiger salamanders lay beneath logs,
called ground cover by all its varied names
spoke 16 languages and read from the books of the dead,
strode with an urgency through urban forests
and took the train to work each day. Tickets, getting
tickets please. Sandwiches in paper bags.

The *aurora borealis* blows through the cells of my bone,
igniting them so that they are torn apart and scattered in the solar wind.
What was it that you wanted to achieve? Why
did we wear our tight shirt collars to expensive hotels
or spend long years sweating our fears into foreign sheets?
I am older now then you were on that day
when you lay down in a blueberry patch and died
on vacation beneath a Minnesota sky.

After the stroke, we had three days before you rose,
and the light in your eyes seemed to go on forever without finding words.
In listening ever since among the stars, I have been paralyzed
and have raised flawed children who are as wise as you
with no desire to pass it on.

In The Plate Glass Window Factory

In the plate glass window factory they watch reflections of sky
and melt down silicon mountains before coffee break.
The sun rises and sets in iron vats.
It is contained.
In the plate glass window factory they build liquid frames
for pictures of farm houses where the farmer rises early in the morning
or for train cars that ensnare the mountains of a continent
and for young women baking bread in little towns of red brick homes.
In the plate glass window factory as the day goes on the breathing hardens
and they pour their crystal lakes into featureless trays
which can be filled with anything,
sweeping time from the floorboards and cutting it out to hang on walls.
And in the plate glass window factory, the workers never go home,
not even when they fish dark rivers beneath the stars.

SPIEL

a surreal incident

shrunken bits of chicken skins lie wasting
on the grey linoleum. the water pan remains untouched.
the old man's long face becomes wan as he shoves
his dry corn flakes from side to side. then with his thumb
he smashes them and empties the bowl onto the floor - -
imagines the comfort of the slapping of her tongue.

he twists his neck as if to suffocate himself - -
attempts, once again, to whisper her familiar name.
but what he hears is the discordant caw of magpies
as they threaten his throat in retaliation for his decision.
flies pester the skins. he is reluctant to slap at them.
he attempts instead to vacuum them up as he putters

about with his old hoover - - poking its nose
into every corner where her brittle hair has mounted
into dust bunnies the size of rats
he presses his nose against the front window. fogs
the glass. waits - - waits - - dozes. scratches his belly.
licks the back of his hand till it is raw pink.

mrs. hollings makes her usual daily visit from next door.
in the shade of the huge cottonwood tree, just ten feet
from the window, she drops bread crusts, a cup of boiled
peas, and some kind of creamy yellow leftovers
his breathing hastens.
he pants and drools.

in the kitchen, he longs to be greeted with a pat
upon his head. the room seems tall and unwelcoming:
her freshly laundered bedsack stinking of harsh detergent - -
neatly folded - - ready to be stashed away in the garage
till he has the gumption to replace her. a well-chewed
green racquetball lies atop her bed.

he bounces the ball off his old black leather slipper, then drops
to his knees to keenly study it as it rolls beneath
the refrigerator. his hand is too large to retrieve
it. the corn flakes and chicken scraps have disappeared.
her water pan has been scrubbed to a steely sheen.
it now holds a banana and two bright red apples. he is thirsty.

he runs to the toilet bowl - - stands over it and stares stupidly
down at his reflection. he suddenly needs to pee.
he trots to the back door and waits - - and waits.
eventually he squats on the carpet but cannot release
his stream. he anxiously watches through the glass patio door
as mrs. hollings' longhaired tomcat struts

along the porch rail, then he returns to the toilet - -
squats - - pees - - places his face into the bowl
and enthusiastically laps up his water. in the dark,
he raids the trash basket. recovers the chicken skins
and wetsopped cereal from among empty containers, wads
of tinfoil, a pork bone, wet newsprint, and the splinters

of a shattered coffee mug. he cuts the tip of his left pinky
finger on the ragged edge of a beefstew can. he licks the blood
off the wound. he is attracted to the odor of the caffeine remains,
wants to consume the bone, but does not wish to dine alone.
he attempts to call out her name, but only the thin yowl
of a coyote, lost in an ancient time, comes forth.

he forgets to rinse the minty toothpaste from his mouth.
a white deposit clings to his lips. his bed seems much too big.
he wrestles his pillows - - kicks furiously at his sheets

till they bind his ankles. a loose mattress spring pokes
his ribs. he is uncomfortable on his belly and cannot
sleep on his back. he struggles to hear the sound of her panting.

the sage's pocket

for all his life
the sage has carried

a stub pencil
a square of paper
a kernel of corn

for when it all falls down - -
to record it

then
replenish the earth
with crop

red bull
for eric

red is black
between your suns
            the bull is red

but this is not
the bull you know

horns of sapphire
testes of light

yesterdays
            between
            your night

the outsider's tongue

without fear
riding bareback
set high upon a wet horse
Thirty degree nights won't kill you

with no reins
this outsider fires his tingue
shooting straight
his words
like the heart of fire

he is drunk with freedom
from the boundaries
that fetter others
to frighten them from saying
what they really would like to say

he ruffles the sober
transfigures eyes of the blind
leaves the complacent bleeding
then - so be it -
jolts his mount to gallop on
to other and more needy climes
while abandoning the meekest
who shudder
behind the shock of revelation:
                fight it or die
                with what they have found

last call

only because we've been companions
for so long
am i able to piece together
what he barely manages
to eke out in frail whispers:

"put...on...a...funny...hat"

so i turn my ballcap inside out
and twist it backwards

"pull my afghan...over...my arms...and
don't...knock my I.V. out of...my...wrist"

a tough call
he is barely skin and bones

"Say...me...that...special poem"

i begin his favorite matthew arnold:
for the world which lies before us
like a land of dreams so various
so beaut...

"Stop kissing my ass"
he mutters

as he closes his eyes
for the final time

JOSEPH VERRILLI

Woman in Various Stages of Redress

1. Today
   She was occupied
   with talking to another man
   by the building's back door
   their banter
   intentionally unintelligible
   the wistful longing
   barely evident
   in her dark eyes
   when she held the door open
   this blustery autumn afternoon

2. Two weeks ago
   She was pulling
   an overloaded box
   to the same back door
   an activity meant to convey
   it belonged exclusively
   to her woman's world
   but seeing her struggling
   something inside me
   told me I should make restitution
   for past infractions
   I picked up the box
   carried it inside
   momentarily preoccupied

with the way her full lips
ascetically complimented
her brown skin

3. Months ago
   The first time I laid eyes
   on her
   in the stuffy laundry room
   the highlight of what I beheld
   were her eyes
   tinted with melancholy
   a disciplined silent longing
   a tragic gaze
   of a recalled restraint
   I decided not to speak
   to her at all
   but couldn't banish
   to forgetfulness
   the way her full lips
   complimented her brown skin
   a saintly countenance
   that should have been captured
   in a stained glass portrait
   from long ago

Ascent
(for Mark Sonnenfeld)

An old photograph
of a young man climbing stairs
springs into view,
unintended fingerprint smudges
dotting the image
almost haphazardly,
shot in the film noir sensibility
of black-and-white starkness.
His hair a bit disheveled,
the eyes looking straight
into the camera lens
with no definable expression,
the background hazy, unclear;
a dream dissolving
upon wakefulness.

If one studies this photograph
long enough,
the available impression
is that the man's ascent
is perfect,
a continual climbing upward,
sometimes slowly,
other times with still purpose.
He is walking up the series of steps,
but is he, really?
His destination eludes
the all-seeing eye of the lens.
Climbing, for all intents and purposes,
becomes a metaphor
for an undisclosed mystery.
Staring out a large window once,
the panoramic view
of the city streets below
almost left him breathless;
this world is mine, he thought.
My observations are for the taking,
to see what others are blind to.
Art is everywhere.
Even in an old, smudged photographg
of a young man climbing stairs,
who retains his own sense of mystery
in a series of thought patterns
ever unfolding.

Pastorale

Shyness was her affliction
surrounded by nervous laughter
whenever someone would tell her
to lift her eyes from the ground
and make eye contact
but everything changes
eventually
her shyness
became a necessary blindness
to see
without the luxury of sight
survival takes many forms

she could rationalize anything

His afflictions were jealousy
a wild imagination
he would accuse her
of sleeping around
even though it wasn't true
then his accusations
became self-fulfilling prophecy
she would become the embodiment
of the Madonna/whore complex
both sensibilities in one body
working in a sex club
the male clients could see her
on the opposite side of the glass
but she could only see
her own reflection
in a gaudy gold-trimmed mirror
the paradox of Western civilization
the man's preoccupation
with viewing the object
without involvement of any kind
this once-shy girl
herded men like sheep
to worship at her shrine
an arid wasteland
fostered by changing mirages

NATHAN WHITING

Clouds Separate

Air behaves for it knows clouds
are its supervisors, the sun the big
investor. Mostly I want to receive
light I can see. The other frequencies
avoid my mind, courts to decide
who can use them and how,
air apparently the same no matter
who wins but secretly air changes
from overuse like a field or a camel.

I seem to bother time barely.
Time must be joyful to be imperiled
so little, though many miss time's
fun as they try each day futilely
to gain a little control.

Lately I've found some unbehaved air
and take lessons to learn how to live
the way it moves in time.
Light travels merrily like riding
a radio into higher frequencies.
Time's own scheme romps invisibly
and stupid clocks just follow time
the way penance follows ecstasy.

Lightning

Lightning strikes and still electricity
through wires prevails. Today's debate
about the death penalty will include accidents,
the kind of accidents we fear.
The experts who discuss lethal directions
appear powerless against hurricane force
odds. Floods bury towns as families fill
their swimming pools. Cars crash.
We enter a new model year.
Better times will include fewer elevator failures
and saner dogs due to animal psychology
few nations can afford. Earths roll but where
are the alternatives, their cruelties from the same
geometry as mine but history can't be chosen.

Other earths don't know us
so we're even. To become as uneven
as we seem, we've had to arrange it.
Are all earth's cleverly governed
by the floors elevators favor
and which animals own animals?
Even plants own other plants.
Can we arrange an earth where no plant
owns a plant and n o elevator has cables?
Lightning strikes. I'd fear
a crazy planet where it didn't.

Decently

A notion may not move me much
for quite a while   he believes
she may be too strong
to touch. Her dress, a summer light
color, slides around her body
as she tells him "You don't quite fit.
Have you thought about a sudden
journey.   I'd like one
but money's not common the way
it was. Neither am I. We both tend
to go where too much precedes us."
He can't ask "May I take your picture
with my phone?"   It sounds
too serious. Life around her does
remember how to play but she
comes as he own referee and he
never understood such hard rules.
The door opens. How?   Oh
her impatience for one kind of air
needs another.   Breath slows
beyond the scent of here.

Ribbons Fail To Shatter

Ribbons of unrepentant steam
linger in deep landscape too private
for eagle devices aimed by the unseen
and curious. Shouts arise
from the fire sale of adamant
believers unable to cool heated want.
They yell from the haze
but their verses can't cut it,
words blunt compared to machine guns
angel thugs use instead of knives.

Brides dangle mile long veils
grooms follow into future.
Halos surround their feet
over ice the origin of vapors
as crowds slide together to slip apart.

A holy disbelief receives light
from a billion light years away.
No entry welcomes the aged message.
No escape greets those just born near.

A Surprise Moves Closer

The best day of the year prepares a surprise.
It might be mature and capable
or infantile and foolish. Before it comes
individuals create complex scenes.
One on her knees goes through discarded books
about travel or maybe she arranges them
by the ways the authors reveal frustration
in their titles. Another lugs a coat
too heavy for his little muscles.
One amid them aims a powerful camera
at a distance. Has the surprise lured him
to capture its delicate approach?

Critics arrive or do they appear to be critics
because they are human? A worry in the air
leaves a few upset but ready for a finer mood,
raw smiles hidden in their cheek pockets.
The surprise appears. It is a beast
of gladness. Not one among us will recall
if it had a form and could be seen.
The photographer looks as if he missed
his true profession, so rocked by excitement
his camera is borrowed by others
who need portraits of themselves shocked.

Gold Or A Kinder Metal

I lost a necklace in light
or light became my necklace
and was stolen. A detective spins,
calculus a substitute for clues,
who did it nobody without a suspect.

The detective views the decorative case
and grins "crowds prove more crooks
exist than laws to help them walk."
Frigid magic rains. I may not want
glitter enough. The detective

fears crime may travel, himself
a cab driver to forgetfulness.
Where did I put the necklace?
I should take better care of the heaven scent
hasty in its azure and lack of dance

by the demi-naked above the bar,
my shadow followed but it never
wears a necklace lit. Snakes crawl
from neon signs and know their hole.
Sirens pass dramas too ornate for names.

Luxury Climbs A Too Steep Dance

Some valleys burn with work
until muscles under dirt evaporate.
Here a tree, her fruit too sharp to share,
has been exiled from the woods.
Nerves drink adrenaline for lunch

then mime tired melodies until hearts
drag lungs to rest, ideology trapped
in ruby waters of skeptical self.
The local deities, not depicted jolly,
alert a distance expectation wants.

Worry traps an extra ritual,
light by the ton stored in dark bones.
Sand into a million boxes between friends,
time borrows energy at its best
from air and ignites explosive euphoria.

The divine gives a bee full of nectar
into mouths slate-heavy with labor
then condemns childish reasons for misery
to swallow vocal flames and sing
when pleasure does my vision, not theirs.

A.D. WINANS

Lucky's Bar

Sitting here at Lucky's Bar
here in the Mission
I eye the one-legged man sitting
on the barstool next to me
His leg blown away by a friend
he burned
A high price to pay for a mistake
His life flowing away in an endless
sea of alcohol

We share a whiskey together
and talk about how long it has been
since he has been with a woman
Fearful for his manhood
and the State paying him a pittance
on disability

Here at Lucky's Bar
Sharing another mans philosophy
Another mans despair
The only beauty he knows
A one oz. shot-glass

The room reeling around me
The glare of knifes descending
on soft flesh
like a surgeon's scalpel grinding
on bone

Words That Bleed

she was the knife in the hands
of Jack the Ripper
in a heavy fog bank
in a back alley in old London Town
slicing and dicing her way through the
canvas of my heart

she was the pearl-handled revolver
in the hands of Dillinger
that begged to be fired
but never had the chance the
night he was gunned down
in a hail of bullets

she was the keg of gunpowder
waiting to be ignited, betrayed
by a wet fuse, the night
I woke naked and vulnerable
feeling like a voyeur walking
in on two strangers making love
my thoughts a mosaic tattoo
on public display
these wounded words that drip blood
lying still as a beached shipwreck
in the bone yard of a stranger's dreams

Woman On The Balcony

I see her two
three times a week
sitting on the balcony
when weather permits
here in old Italy town
in what is left of North Beach
her robe slightly parted with sensual
thoughts left to the imagination
thumbing through the pages of a book
taking no notice of the people down below

standing to stretch, she yawns
legs like sturdy pillars that stretch
to reach the sky into the boundaries
of my mind
my eyes begging to read the pages
she turns with sensual fingers
wanting just one quick look
one intimate journey into the pages
into the space between the
parting of her robe
a journey to forbidden places

a flight back in time
to another place another world
high on a balcony where
I too ignore the
people coming and going
down below

Digital Age

I told you not to take a snapshot
I don't photograph well
But you did nevertheless
And sent it to me by means of attachment
And there it was on the screen
In black and white the only colors that matter
And it split into two parts on the screen
Neither of them doing me justice
An injustice I am sure not intended
This faceless face staring back at me
Smashed into a thousand lines
This snapshot more like an empty face
Stuffed away in a shoebox
In the far corner of a closet
Like a series of quick winks lost
In cyber space

Winter Poem

It's been in the thirties
two nights in a row
and I'm sitting here freezing
my butt off with a hacking cough
waiting for the power company
to come and fix the problem
but it isn't so bad
when you consider 9/11
the war on Iraq
and that d.a. levy
took a rifle between his legs
and blew his brains out
which has nothing and yet everything
to do with this poem

but they don't bring comfort either
the trouble with being single
the trouble with being seventy
is knowing you could die alone
and go undiscovered for weeks
with nothing but rotting flesh
to tell your story
and a few poems to remember
you by

On Why I Dislike Marin

Six-and-one half months since the
Fire at my San Francisco apartment
And my staying with my sister in Marin
          (Corte Madera to be exact)

Depressed and suffering from another
Night of chronic insomnia
I head for the mall and Tully's Coffee Shop
For a cup of coffee to wire my numbed
Brain cells.

I enter the door and find two Yuppie women
Ahead of me in line
Dressed in $200 designer jeans
          (I kid you not)
Each of them with a child in an expensive stroller
Oblivious to my existence

The first woman finally pulls out a $100 bill
And asks the minimum wage kid
"Can you change this?"
And he nods his head yes and hands her back
$96 in change
          (She doesn't drink regular coffee)

She puts the change in her purse without
So much as a thank you
And leaves no tip

The second woman hands the clerk a $50 bill
        (I haven't seen one of those in ages)
Again, no thank you and no tip

I watch them head for a corner table the
First woman bitching about the stock market
Saying she lost $7,000 in one day
Her friend saying, "I know
My stock portfolio shows only a 7% profit
For the year"

These are what are known as Marinites
Who drive BMW's, SUV's and Sport Cars
They walk the Garden of Eden
Looking for the tastiest and most expensive apple
Daintily spitting out the seeds into silk handkerchiefs
Living their lives in a suicide pact
With themselves

Winter Poem Three

Chill of winter in the air
Misty fog giving way
To a light rain
Cars spewing deadly exhaust fumes
Windshield wipers flapping like the
Wings of birds in migration
Stone faces hidden behind steering wheels
Give no quarter yield only to the
Red traffic stoplights
Pedestrians looking like mannequins
Turn into penguins scurrying
Across the street
On their way to work
Boarding the morning bus
Pressed together like preserved butterflies
Between the pages of an old
And frayed book

Blue Café

Blues-chilling
Jamming-trio
Be-bopping
Toe-snapping jazz
God giving the devil his due
Here at the Cafe Blue
Hip swinging Ma-Ma
Strutting her stuff
On the dance floor
Lip-smacking gun-packing poems
Court fire-breathing demons
Riding my optic nerves
Blinking like a world class
Pinball machine

Contributors

(Includes year of birth, current state of residence, followed by most recent book & some of the literary journals that publish the poets work.)

JOHN AMEN, *b. 1966*. North Carolina. *At the Threshold of Alchemy* (Presa Press, 2009). *Adironack Review, Gargoyle, The New York Quarterly, Paterson Literary Review, Rattle.* Editor of *The Pedestal*.

ANTLER, *b. 1946*. Wisconsin. *Boy Talking in His Sleep* (Shivastan Press, forthcoming). *Against Armageddon, Cost of Freedom, Earth Blessings, The New York Quarterly, Wilderness Blessings.*

GUY BEINING, *b. 1938*. Massachusetts. *Inrue* (Phrygian Press, 2008). *Chiron Review, Edgz, Epicenter, Quercus Review, Skidrow Penthouse.*

ALAN CATLIN, *b. 1948*. New York. *The Insomniac's Dream* (Shark Art, forthcoming). *5AM, Aurorean, Chiron Review, Iodine Poetry Journal, Main Street Rag.*

DAVID CHORLTON, *b. 1948*. Arizona. *The Lost River* (Rain Mountain Press, 2008). *Avocet, Chiron Review, Public Republic, Third Wednesday, Voices on the Wind.*

KIRBY CONGDON, *b. 1924*. Florida. *Untitled* (Marymark Press, forthcoming). *The Christian Science Monitor, The Colorado Quarterly, Home Planet News, Iconoclast, The New York Times.* Editor of *Magazine*.

DAVID COPE, *b. 1948*. Michigan. *Turn The Wheel* (Humana Press, 2003). *Chiron Review, The New York Quarterly, Paterson Literary Review, Rattapallax, Van Gogh's Ear.* Editor of *Big Scream*.

JOHN ELSBERG, *b. 1945*. Virginia. *South Jersey Shore: Poems and Brief Sketches* (with David Check, Bogg Publications, 2005). *The Broadkill Review, Chiron Review, Edgz, Modern Haiku.* Editor of *Bogg: A Journal of Contemporary Writing*.

JEAN ESTEVE, *b. 1929*. Oregon. *Iowa Review, Main Street Rag, Median, Pleiades.*

MICHAEL FLANAGAN, *b. 1963*. Virginia. *A Million Years Gone* (Liquid Paper Press, 2008). *Barbaric Yawp, Home Planet News, The New York Quarterly, Quercus Review, Slipstream.*

HUGH FOX, *b. 1932*. Michigan. *Icehouse and The Thirteen Keys To Talmud* (Chaos Crossing Press, 2009). *Gargoyle, Home Planet News, Poetica, Tears In The Fence, Wilderness House Literary Review.* Contributing Editor of *Presa*.

ERIC GREINKE, *b. 1948*. Michigan. *Wild Strawberries* (Presa Press, 2008). *California Quarterly, Chiron Review, HazMat Review, The New York Quarterly, The Pedestal.* Contributing Editor of *Presa*.

JOHN GREY, *b. 1954*. Rhode Island. *What Else Is There (*Main Street Rag, 2004). *Art Mag, Blueline, Connecticut Review, Ekphrasis, Georgetown Review.*

CAROL HAMILTON, *b. 1935.* Oklahoma. *Shots On* (Finishing Line Press, 2008). *Atlanta Review, Bogg, California Quarterly, Mad Poets Review, The New York Quarterly.*

DOUG HOLDER, *b. 1955*. Massachusetts. *From the Paris of New England: Interviews with Poets and Writers* (Ibbetson Street Press, 2009). *Endicott Review, Long Island Quarterly, Oak Bend Review, Wilderness House Literary Review.* Editor of *Ibbeston Street.*

ROBERT K. JOHNSON *b. 1932*. Massachusetts. *From Mist To Shadow* (Ibbetson Street Press, 2007). *Main Channel Voices, The New York Times, Pegasus, The Poetry Porch, Slipstream.*

ARTHUR WINFIELD KNIGHT, *b. 1937*. Nevada. *Misfits Country* (Tres Picos Press, 2008). *The New York Quarterly, Poet Lore, Windsor Review.*

RONNIE M. LANE, *b. 1949*. Michigan. *Carolina Journal* (Free Books, 2008). *Big Scream, Crossing Rivers Into Twilight, Neonbeam, University of Tampa Review, Voices.*

DONALD LEV, *b. 1936*. New York. *The Darkness Above: Selected Poems 1968-2002* (Red Hill Outloudbooks, 2008). *Big Hammer, Chiron Review, The New York Quarterly, Tribes, Waterways.* Editor of *Home Planet News.*

LYN LIFSHIN, *b. 1944*. Virginia. *Light At The End* (Clevis Hook Press, 2008). *HazMat Review, Home Planet News, Mad Poets Review, New Letters, The New York Quarterly, Paterson Literary Review.*

ELLARAINE LOCKIE, *b. 1945*. California. *Blue Ribbons at the County Fair* (PWJ Publishing, 2008). *Chiron Review, Georgetown Review, Ibbetson Street, Iconoclast, Main Street Rag.*

GERALD LOCKLIN, *b. 1941*. California. *Gerald Locklin: New and Selected Poems* (World Parade Books, 2008). *Ambit, Freefall, The New York Quarterly, Slipstream, Tears In The Fence.* Editor of *Chiron Review.*

B.Z. NIDITCH, *b. 1943*. Massachusetts. *Portraits* (Alternating Current/Propaganda Press, 2008). *Antioch Review, Denver Quarterly, Hawaii Review, The Literary Review, Prairie Schooner.*

SIMON PERCHIK, *b. 1923.* New York. *Family of Man* (Pavement Saw Press, forthcoming). *Agni, American Letters & Commentary, Beloit Poetry Journal, Colorado Review, Northwest Review.*

CHARLES P. RIES, *b. 1952*. Wisconsin. *Girl Friend & Other Mysteries of Love* (Alternating Current /Propaganda Press, forthcoming). *Bathtub Gin, Clark Street Review, HazMat Review, Iconoclast, Lummox Journal.* Editor of *Word Riot.*

LYNNE SAVITT, *b. 1947*. New York. *Digging Dinosaur Dignity In Ardortown* (Myshkin Press, 2008). *Butcherblock, Chiron Review, Lummox, The New York Quarterly, Playgirl.*

HARRY SMITH, *b. 1936.* Maine. *Little Things* (Presa Press, 2009). *Confrontation, Iconoclast, The Pedestal, Prairie Schooner, Solo Café.* Contributing Editor of *Presa.*

JARED SMITH, *b. 1950.* Colorado. *Selected Longer Poems: 1984-2008* (Tamarack Editions, forthcoming). *Home Planet News, The New York Quarterly, The Pedestal, The Toronto Quarterly, Wilderness House Literary Review.*

SPIEL, *b. 1941.* Colorado. *she: insinuations of flesh brooding* (March Street Press, 2008). *Alpha Beat Soup, First Class, Free Verse, Slipstream, Zygote in My Coffee.*

JOSEPH VERRILLI, *b. 1952.* Connecticut. *Body English* (Alternating Current/Propaganda Press, 2009). *The Brown Bottle, Chiron Review, Poesy, Zen Baby.* Editor of *Drama Garden.*

NATHAN WHITING, *b. 1946.* New York. *I a Hen Guard Myself by Me a Fox* (Moon Press, 2007). *The 13ᵗʰ Warrior Review, The New York Quarterly, Pudding Magazine, Salamander.*

A.D. WINANS, *b. 1936.* California. *Marking Time* (Erbacca Press, 2008). *Beat Scene, Global Tapestry, Home Planet News, Main Street Rag, The New York Quarterly.* Editor of *Second Coming.*

Also Available From Presa Press

At the Threshold of Alchemy - **John Amen**
ISBN: 978-0-9800081-5-9; 86 pgs.; pp; $13.95.

The Rebel - Poems By Charles Baudelaire
American versions by Leslie H. Whitten Jr.
48 pgs.; ssp; $7.00.

Alice - **Louis E. Bourgeois**
40 pgs.; ssp; $6.00.

God Is Dead (again) - **Kirby Congdon**
ISBN: 978-0-9772524-2-8; 120 pgs.; pp; $20.00.

Selected Poems & Prose Poems - **Kirby Congdon**
ISBN: 978-0-9772524-0-4; 84 pgs.; pp; $15.00.

Blood Cocoon - Selected Poems Of Connie Fox - **Hugh Fox**
ISBN: 978-0-9740868-9-7; 72 pgs.; pp; $15.00.

Time & Other Poems - **Hugh Fox**
44 pgs.; ssp; $6.00.

Selected Poems 1972-2005 - **Eric Greinke**
ISBN: 978-0-9740868-7-3; 140 pgs.; pp; $20.00.

Wild Strawberries - **Eric Greinke**
ISBN: 978-0-9800081-1-1; 96 pgs.; pp; $15.00.

The Burning Mirror - **Kerry Shawn Keys**
ISBN: 978-0-9772524-9-7; 92 pgs.; pp; $14.95.

Book Of Beasts - **Kerry Shawn Keys**
ISBN: 978-0-9800081-4-2; 64 pgs.; pp; $13.95.

PO/EMS - **Richard Kostelanetz**
40 pgs.; ssp; $6.00.

Morpheus Rising - **Ronnie M. Lane**
40 pgs.; ssp; $6.00.

Living In Dangerous Times - **Linda Lerner**
52 pgs.; ssp; $6.00.

In Mirrors - **Lyn Lifshin**
ISBN: 978-0-9772524-3-5; 84 pgs.; pp; $15.00.

Seedpods - **Glenna Luschei**
40 pgs.; ssp; $6.00.

Total Immersion - **Glenna Luschei**
ISBN: 978-0-9800081-0-4; 96 pgs.; pp; $15.00.

Pre-Socratic Points & Other New Poems - **Stanley Nelson**
ISBN: 978-0-9772524-4-2; 84 pgs.; pp; $15.00.

Limbos For Amplified Harpsichord - **Stanley Nelson**
ISBN: 978-0-9772524-8-0; 144 pgs.; pp; $17.95.

City Of The Sun - **Stanley Nelson**
ISBN: 978-0-9800081-2-8; 126 pgs.; pp; $15.95.

The Drunken Boat & Other Poems From The French Of Arthur Rimbaud - **American versions by Eric Greinke**
ISBN: 978-0-9772524-7-3; 108 pgs.; pp; Bi-lingual edition; $15.95.

Inside The Outside - An Anthology Of Avant-Garde American Poets **Edited by Roseanne Ritzema**
ISBN: 978-0-9772524-1-1; 304 pgs.; pp; $29.95.

The Deployment Of Love In Pineapple Twilight - **Lynne Savitt**
48 pgs.; ssp; $6.00.

Up North - **Harry Smith & Eric Greinke**
40 pgs.; ssp; $6.00.

Little Things - **Harry Smith**
ISBN: 978-9800081-3-5; 78 pgs.; pp; $13.95.

This Land Is Not My Land - **A.D. Winans**
48 pgs.; ssp; $6.00.

The Other Side Of Broadway: Selected Poems:1965-2005 - **A.D. Winans;**
ISBN: 978-0-9772524-5-9; 132 pgs.; pp; $18.00.

Available through Baker & Taylor, The Book House, Coutts Information Services, Midwest Library Services, www.amazon.com, www.bn.com, www.thelostbookshelf,.com & directly through the publisher - **www.presapress.com**

Exclusive European distribution through Gazelle Book Service Ltd. (UK)
sales@gazellebooks.co.uk   www.gazellebooks.co.uk